HOW WOMEN WORK

Celebrating
30 Years of Publishing
in India

Praise for *How Women Work*

Aarti Kelshikar does a masterful job of exploring the varied experiences, challenges and triumphs of female leaders in Asia. I learnt so much from reading this book and would highly recommend it for anyone interested in understanding female leadership in one of the most important regions in the world.

—**Andy Molinsky**, PhD, author of *Global Dexterity* and *Reach*

How Women Work: Fitting In and Standing Out in Asia sheds light on how women lead in different cultural contexts and come out as winners. It explains how they navigate their professional journeys, adopting strategies and skills that are relevant in a complex global world. It is an insightful book on the way women engage and practice leadership. Women are naturally intuitive, can discern patterns and draw insights, and connect the dots!

—**Nandan Nilekani**, chairman and co-founder, Infosys and founding chairman, UIDAI

A new trailblazing book by Aarti Kelshikar! In *How India Works*, she was the first to tell us about the cultural nuances of doing business in India. In *How Women Work*, she gives a voice to women leaders in Asia for the first time. This book encapsulates all the wisdom and experience of women leaders who have walked the talk. It's a book for the next generation of women who dream to lead Asia and the world.

—**Dr Catherine Wu**, Center for Leadership and Cultural Intelligence, Nanyang Technological University, Singapore

A book for these VUCA times, *How Women Work: Fitting In and Standing Out in Asia* offers great insights from female business leaders across diverse Asia cultures who share their experiences, and provide valuable tips on how they drive successful outcomes in their business and/or professional journeys. It covers myriad topics and is filled with useful advice on everyday challenges many women face in the workplace. *How Women Work* is a must-read for anyone who wants to be successful in Asia business.

—**Geraldine Kor**, managing director, South Asia and head of Global Enterprise, Telstra

Aarti Kelshikar picks an important theme that discusses the topic of 'women in the workplace', examines it from the prism of Asia for its nuances and unique sub-cultures, does a series of insightful interviews with accomplished women leaders from several countries in Asia across a variety of work arenas and then distils the messages from these leaders into themes that help us all become better women leaders or allies to women in the Asian workplace.

—**Madhav Kalyan**, managing director, APAC Head of Payments, J.P. Morgan

How Women Work is a fascinating deep dive into the journeys of women leaders from different cultural contexts. It highlights the resilience and adaptability of women in this region.

The book goes beyond the theme of women's leadership. Aarti has woven in the topic of working effectively across cultures.

How Women Work is layered with interesting nuances and useful insights that are valuable for anyone looking to do business in this region.

—**Joyce Jenkins**, managing partner, director of Programmes at Expert Humans, Singapore and founder of Society for Intercultural Education, Training and Research (SIETAR) Southeast Asia

Aarti skilfully explores the myriad ways in which Asian women navigate the nuances of the corporate world amidst the cultural subtext.

Unpretentious and candid, *How Women Work* unravels facets that are commonly experienced but seldom found in a book on women's leadership in Asia. In today's global, boundary-less world, this book is a must-read for everyone and I personally would recommend having 'been there and seen it all'.

—**Ranjana Maitra**, country head, University of New Haven India & SE Asia, and co-chair of Western region, Confederation of Indian Industry (CII), Indian Women's Network

How Women Work: Fitting In and Standing Out in Asia is a book not to be missed. It explores how Asian women work, lead and succeed. And how women leaders, through connection, communication, collaboration and contribution, take control of how they want to fit in and when they want to stand out.

—**Kim Underhill**, CEO, The SHE BRILLIANCE Movement

How Women Work: Fitting In and Standing Out in Asia is an excellent account of women leadership in the corporate world in Asia. The book highlights how women leaders successfully navigate varied situations and contexts. We need to celebrate women in all walks of life and I certainly do my bit in sport!

—**Ajit Agarkar**, Indian cricketer and commentator

Aarti Kelshikar's latest book offers a roadmap into leadership lessons, engaging the reader with relatable stories from women around the region. Each chapter pulls you in with an anecdote designed to illustrate a theme in leadership.

The intertwining of gender and culture offers a nuanced peek into the challenges and opportunities that many leaders face on a regular basis. In this book, Aarti offers insight into common themes of cultural context while honouring and recognizing the rich diversity and complexity of the continent.

—**Nada Collins**, PhD, superintendent, Asociación Escuelas Lincoln, Argentina

If as they say 'the future is female' then *How Women Work* is a must-read. The author beautifully uncovers how women in Asia navigate the leadership track, through a series of revelatory interviews.

—**Dr Payal Kumar**, principal academic advisor, ISH, India, author of *Gender Equity in The Boardroom: The Case of India*

HOW WOMEN WORK

Fitting In and Standing Out in Asia

AARTI KELSHIKAR

HarperCollins *Publishers* India

First published in India by HarperCollins *Publishers* 2023
4th Floor, Tower A, Building No. 10, DLF Cyber City,
DLF Phase II, Gurugram, Haryana – 122002
www.harpercollins.co.in

2 4 6 8 10 9 7 5 3 1

Copyright © Aarti Kelshikar 2023

P-ISBN: 978-93-5629-585-8
E-ISBN: 978-93-5629-586-5

The views and opinions expressed in this book are the author's own and the facts are as reported by her, and the publishers are not in any way liable for the same.

Aarti Kelshikar asserts the moral right
to be identified as the author of this work.

All rights reserved. No part of this publication may be reproduced, stored in a retrieval system, or transmitted, in any form or by any means, electronic, mechanical, photocopying, recording or otherwise, without the prior permission of the publishers.

Typeset in 11/15.5 Galliard BT at
Manipal Technologies Limited, Manipal

Printed and bound at
Replika Press Pvt. Ltd.

This book is produced from independently certified FSC® paper to ensure responsible forest management.

For

my father, Dilip Phatarphekar

who lived and led

with love and laughter.

Contents

Introduction	xiii
1. A Sliver of Culture	1
2. Courage and Control	22
3. Results and Relationships	40
4. Connecting the Dots	57
5. Trust and Credibility	74
6. Fitting In and Standing Out	96
7. Visible and Vocal	112
8. The Good Women of Asia	129
9. Don't Talk Like a B@#$%	148
10. Reach and Resilience	163
11. How They Lead	178
12. More or Less	198
Conclusion	202
Additional References	209
Interviewee Profiles	215
Acknowledgements	227
Index	231
About the Author	239

Introduction

'Asia: The future is female.' This was the title of an article I came across a few years ago in *The Straits Times*, Singapore's leading newspaper.[1] A thought-provoking title, it struck me as being a timely and relevant theme to explore and write a book about. The article intrigued and excited me in equal measure, raising questions on areas that I discuss in this book.

While there is much literature on women in leadership and how to engage, lead and lean in, it is largely through a Western lens. *How Women Work: Fitting In and Standing Out in Asia* pays homage to women's outstanding success in this part of the world, as seen through an Asian lens.

---

1 Sri Mulyani Indrawati and Anne-Birgitte Albrectsen, 'Asia: The future is female', *The Straits Times*, 8 September 2018

Asia is complex and continues to evolve. On one hand, many Asian countries display broad cultural preferences such as respect for hierarchy and tradition. Harmony and humility are placed at a premium. Patriarchal mindsets are prevalent, and in many places, women are still expected to fulfil their primary responsibility of looking after their home and hearth. Yet, there are women who run dynamic businesses and have successful corporate careers. This book examines what it means to be a successful woman leader against the backdrop of these cultural values.

When I first mentioned to friends that I was going to write a book on women in Asia, there was much excitement. Almost everyone thought it was an interesting topic and had a suggestion on what areas I should focus on. My initial thought was to work with a theme on the lines of 'The Good Women of Asia'. When I mentioned this to friends, I was asked probing questions on what I meant by 'good' women. I explained that this tentative title related to the ingrained mindset in many Asian countries where women are expected to behave a certain way and to be good daughters, wives, mothers and colleagues. I wanted to take a look at women's success through the prism of sociocultural values, a theme close to my heart and professional interest.

But Asia cannot be painted with a single brush. There are nuances in different hues and shapes that dot the cultural landscape. In addition to the universal challenges that women in the workplace encounter, this book takes a look at how cultural values and conditioning in this part of the world impact women in terms of the way they work, lead, communicate and succeed. The narrative is a compilation of women's success and leadership laced with cultural insights across the countries of Singapore, India, China, Japan, Thailand and the Philippines.

Some of the themes that are discussed in this book relate to what women do, differently perhaps, in terms of building credibility and trust, communicating tough decisions and managing teams. We also celebrate the best of women in leadership, in terms of fleshing out some attributes that facilitate their success and help sustain their drive. Additionally, we discuss what works and what doesn't work across parts of Asia and how women leverage their strengths and work around the gaps.

How Women Work attempts to address questions like are the rules defining women leaders in Asia unique or different from those prevalent elsewhere and if so, in what ways? What are some perceptions and biases that working women encounter and, importantly, how have successful women navigated these mindsets?

While working on this book, I spoke with leaders—men and women—from China, Japan, Thailand, Taiwan, Singapore, India, Philippines, Indonesia, Hong Kong and Sri Lanka. I also spoke with some expatriates who had lived in Asia. Many of the women are senior leaders, directors or CEOs of multinational corporations or local organizations. I had conversations with experienced HR executives, consultants and entrepreneurs who run family businesses. I also spoke with a few millennial women founders of businesses. The conversations with women leaders helped paint an insider perspective whereas the conversations with male leaders provide an outsider perspective. Both sets of perspectives—one experienced and lived, the other observed—are relevant and help connect the dots for this book.

I have endeavoured to distil and synthesize these varied observations and experiences to provide a balanced perspective, which I believe is one of the highlights of this book.

An ode to what women do well, and celebrating how they rise and shine, the book has stories of success and struggle. Contained here is an interesting assimilation of personal accounts and real-life experiences from China to India and Japan to Thailand. This is such a dynamic and diverse region with many lessons to offer. As one of my interviewees mentioned, 'this book provides a collective perspective' of diverse women's voices and journeys.

If leadership traits are gender-agnostic, the question that arises is what is the need for a book about women's leadership? For women in the workplace, the starting point is different, the journey is riddled with unique challenges, and the end point doesn't look the same. That's the reality for many women across the globe; the intention is not to single out gender for its own sake. Also, while working on the book, I realized that men and women in a corporate world or as entrepreneurs who haven't seen or experienced the struggle or the biases first-hand can be blasé about this book's premise and the larger theme.

How Women Work is a compilation of the lessons to live and work by for both women and men. While some of the stories are as seen and narrated through a female perspective, they are certainly relevant and relatable to a larger audience. *How Women Work* is about leaders who are also women; it encapsulates the good, bad and ugly of what *that* entails. The idea is to enable a sense of appreciation about the journey and outline what it takes to get there—this book has been a step in that direction.

The book explores the significance of 'good women' in contemporary times, given the prevalence of women who push boundaries and live life on their terms. The reader may find that some themes overlap in the book; leadership traits can't be compartmentalized in tight boxes sealed with a bow!

How Women Work also contains lessons and tips to navigate working across countries and cultures. While there may be less overseas travel and in-person meetings in the near future, these learnings would still be relevant in a world where connecting virtually has unique complexities.

Importantly, the book provides a unique perspective from someone who is both an outsider and yet has experienced many of the themes discussed in the book. As someone who has had the opportunity to wear different hats and reinvent the wheel, I know a thing or two about success and failure, learning and evolving, skills and mindsets. I have worked as a manager in India's apex regulatory body for capital markets and as a consultant in a compliance-based firm in Singapore. I have worked in the intercultural coaching space since 2008 and have conducted several workshops and training programmes enabling senior executives to work more effectively across cultures—both organizational and geographic. A few years ago, I wrote a non-fiction book titled *How India Works: Making Sense of a Complex Corporate Culture*. The book is a guide on navigating the complex cultural nuances that working in India, and with Indians, entails. This journey for a first-time author from ideation to publication was enriching and exciting. And during the past two years of the pandemic, I researched and wrote this book. I also founded my company in the intercultural consulting space.

I may not be *successful* in terms of the conventional definition, but I consider myself richer for my learnings and varied experiences. I bring to the table a fresh approach and style in the way this book has been conceptualized and written, as compared to other books on the same subject. I am familiar with and have experienced many of the themes discussed in these pages. I have seen first-hand the importance of 'being visible and vocal' and understand what 'gaining trust' and 'establishing credibility' entail. 'How to fit in and stand out' may be a cliché, but it touches a chord on many levels.

The narrative in the pages ahead is intertwined with insights on culture and leadership, lending the book a unique depth and breadth. These are no easy answers or formulaic solutions but by sharing the practical ways in which women leaders effectively work and lead, there are lessons and learnings for both men and women.

It should be noted that that all statements shared by the people quoted in the book are made in a personal capacity.

Also, I would like to clarify that there is no intent to stereotype or exaggerate how a certain culture works. The intention is to provide and enable an insightful, balanced and interesting perspective. And it is sprinkled with humour wherever possible, because this book, like life, is meant to be savoured and learnt from!

1
A Sliver of Culture

Asia is both 'emerging' and 'developed', embracing technology and tradition against a backdrop of practices and beliefs that have been carried forth and distilled over time. At the workplace, the dynamics of hierarchy, title and age play out in terms of how one behaves and is expected to behave.

Let's take the example of Arisa,[2] a senior leader of Thai origin who spent her formative years in Europe and moved back to Thailand some years ago. It's interesting to hear her impressions when she moved back 'home' and how she dealt with the cultural nuances of her country of origin:

> When I started work in a Thai company, the first thing that struck me was the importance of hierarchy in terms of the organization structure. Despite being in my mid-thirties, I had a senior role, which people respected. It was a bit of

---

2 Name changed to protect privacy.

a culture shock to see how my colleagues would perceive anything I said as sacred and immediately try to follow it, even if it was an offhand comment!

While my title gave me status in the organization, I needed to be cognizant that age also mattered. For instance, when I didn't do a *wai* (the Thai greeting) to one of my colleagues, it was seen as not showing respect to an older colleague who was a long-timer in the organization. Respect was displayed in salutations such as 'khun' and 'phi' for an older person and 'nong' for a younger one. Initially, I would feel uncomfortable when people would call me by these greetings; I was used to working in professional environments where people addressed me by my name and not according to one's age.

Over time, I have learnt that these salutations are a good way of building and fostering relationships. In my first introduction with clients I use *khun* but when I use the prefix of *phi* and *nong*, I know that having switched to a working relationship, things will move faster. The Western approach is about being focused on goals and objectives while working. In Thailand, however, the workday is a mix of work, building relationships and personal chit-chat. That's how things get done.

This example illustrates a few of the nuances that one experiences in this part of the world. After the initial culture shock on 'coming home', Arisa was able to adapt gradually to the ways of working. In the example above, *phi* and *nong* are salutations; *phi* means elder brother or sister, while *nong* means younger brother or sister. In a more formal situation, the word *khun* is used (meaning 'you') to address a person.

In much of Asia, hierarchy rears its head or, literally speaking, lowers it in different ways. In Japan, people bow. In Thailand, they fold hands in the traditional *wai* greeting. In Singapore and India, when meeting an older person socially, the conversation is almost always prefaced with a greeting of 'uncle' or 'auntie'. Indicative of the broader societal values, these are but a few behaviours that manifest respect and deference.

While hierarchy is prevalent, so is the need to connect and forge trust with people in the personal, social and professional spaces. Given the importance of harmony and 'saving face', people tend to avoid conflict and confrontation in general.

A common thread across some of these cultures is that people are reticent and often underplay their achievements. Humility is a virtue and a value.

The influence of Confucianism, an ancient Chinese belief system based on the teachings of Confucius, a philosopher and teacher, is evident across much of East Asia and Singapore. One of the tenets of Confucianism relates to the stability of society, which is based on unequal relationships between people such as father–son, older brother–younger brother and husband–wife. These relationships, based on mutual obligations, underline and impact the prevalence of hierarchy in society.

Speaking of values and priorities, the family is an integral part of the Asian ecosystem. The concept of filial piety often results in family obligations taking precedence over personal responsibilities or interests. The family is a source of huge support for working women in Asia, with the ecosystem often extending to grandparents and helpers. This set-up enables women to work and travel with greater ease and flexibility.

Broadly speaking, while these overarching nuances are prevalent in much of Asia, they differ in subtle and not-so-subtle ways across countries. I have attempted to provide a sliver of the cultural and gender dynamics of six Asian countries here, namely, the Philippines, China, Singapore, Thailand, Japan and India. Needless to say, this needs to be seen in the context of their socio-economic, historical and political contexts.

The country-specific descriptions in this chapter are not a commentary on the society, government or laws of any country. They are shaped by my observations and experiences, as well as of those of my interlocutors.

Philippines

'It's more fun in the Philippines' was a popular tagline for an advertisement when my family and I were living there, something I can attest to. A culture of making the most of 'the here and now', Filipinos have a zest for life, which may be attributed to their Spanish influences.

The Philippines has a long history of colonization; it was under Spanish rule and subsequently under American rule for several years. Given this and the political history post-independence, Filipinos or Pinoys, as they are known, are accepting and respectful of power and authority. They often use the salutation 'po', which denotes respect, when greeting people.

Their helpful nature and willingness to go the extra mile are some factors for the huge success of industries such as business process outsourcing (BPO) in the Philippines. I recently heard how, in a call centre in the BPO space, they place a mirror in front of the tele-operators/agents reminding them to smile! This, in a country known for its friendly faces and warm welcomes.

Filipinos are relationship-oriented, and there is much camaraderie at the workplace. They believe in the concept of *pakikisama*, which relates to fostering a sense of bonding and being a part of a community. Polite to a fault, Filipinos tend to go out of their way to avoid losing face or causing others to lose face. They are cognizant of *hiya*, a value that is related to a person's sense of self-esteem or how others see a person.

From a gender standpoint, it is a progressive society where women are given equal opportunities in education and jobs. Working women, including single mothers, are encouraged to work, and their children are looked after by the family with parents, in-laws and grandparents pitching in.

In the Philippines in general, there are more women in the workforce than men; it is not unusual to see women occupying middle- to senior-level positions in organizations.

This is corroborated in Grant Thornton International's Women in Business report[3] which showed that in 2021, women held 48 per cent of senior management positions in the Philippines. This places the Philippines in the number one position as the country with most women in senior management in mid-market businesses in 2021.

China

From all accounts, China, with a high score on the power distance index (PDI) of the Hofstede model of cultural dimensions, is considered a hierarchical society. PDI, which ranges from 1 to 100, is an indicator of how hierarchical a society is. To put this in context, Austria and Israel have the lowest PDI scores of 11 and 13, respectively, whereas Malaysia scores very high with a PDI score of 100. China, with a score of 80, is on the higher side of this scale. To clarify, these scores are not an accurate representation of all situations and individuals but they do provide an initial comparative picture of where a country stands on certain parameters.

---

3 'Bernie Cahiles-Magkilat, 'PH retains top rank in senior leadership positions', Manila Bulletin, 23 February 2021 (mb.com.ph)

> ## Hofstede's Cultural Dimensions Model
>
> Professor Geert Hofstede, a Dutch social psychologist, developed a six-dimensional model explaining differences between national cultures. The six dimensions are:
>
> - Power Distance Index: the degree of inequality that exists and is accepted in a society
> - Individualism vs Collectivism: the strength of ties that people have to others within their community
> - Masculinity vs Femininity: the distribution of roles between men and women
> - Uncertainty Avoidance Index: how a country handles uncertain events and can cope with anxiety
> - Long-term vs Short-term Orientation: the time horizon people in a society display
> - Indulgence vs Restraint: the extent to which a society encourages gratification of people's drives and emotions
>
> *Source*: MindTools, https://www.mindtools.com/pages/article/newLDR_66.htm

China is also considered to be a masculine society, another dimension in the Hofstede framework, which indicates its success-orientation and driven characteristics. Notwithstanding these parameters, leadership is largely considered to be gender-neutral in China. Especially in New Age industries such as technology-based start-ups in education and other areas, there are many female founders and leaders.

From an outsider's perspective, Chinese women are much higher on the equality metric as compared to women from some other Asian countries. This is largely attributed to Mao Zedong's initial efforts to encourage more women to join the labour force.

While Mao Zedong is associated with the excesses of mass mobilization campaigns such as the Great Leap Forward and the Cultural Revolution, he also challenged gender norms.[4] He promulgated that 'women hold up half the sky' in order to encourage women to work outside the home and boost national productivity.

Chinese women are tenacious and work long hours. Whether it's in a factory or a restaurant, Chinese women have the capacity and ability to work incredibly hard. Historically, the one-child policy has enabled working women to have considerable parental support to look after their kids. As Mike Liu, the former managing director and legal representative for DXC Technology in the Greater China region says, 'They do not have any fears nor insecurity in themselves in the professional workplace because of their gender. They are passionate about building equity in society.'

One reason for Chinese women being successful in business is attributed to the huge economic growth and consequently the opportunities it brought about for men and women alike. Many successful women built their acumen and skills initially in state-owned enterprises.[5]

---

4 https://www.noemamag.com/i-would-rather-be-born-a-woman-in-china-than-india, Pallavi Aiyer, 'I would rather be born a woman in China than India', *Noemag.com*, 19 January 2021

5 Aileen Jung and Cecilia Wang, Women Entrepreneurship in China: Past, Present, and Future, *Fair Observer*, 20 August 2012

Chinese women are hugely entrepreneurial and successful; as per reports, they constitute 70 per cent of the world's most successful women entrepreneurs. Also, China's eighty-five female billionaires amount to two-thirds of the 130 women billionaires in the world.[6]

Mao's thrust was aimed at levelling the playing field in China, quite literally. However, in practice, it was difficult for policies and measures to change deeply ingrained social practices. So, while women are visible and successful, home and hearth continue to primarily be their responsibility. As Chinese publisher and author Xu Ge Fei says: 'In theory, women are equal and have rights like the right to buy property, to trade and to create a company. Yet these freedoms come at enormous responsibility, which women have to shoulder. You have to be three superwomen at the same time to manage home, hearth and all expectations. So yes, we are *half the sky* but the half sky is applied on a different value chain!'

Singapore

In Singapore, the premise is about being perfect. Given that the cost of living is high, a double income is often considered necessary to live well and comfortably. This pragmatism, amongst other factors, underlies the gender inclusive approach at the workplace.

Success is defined in terms of working hard, which is common, as is stress on account of work. As per a survey by health service company Cigna in 2019, nearly 92 per cent of Singaporeans

---

6 Qin Chen, 'China is now home to two-thirds of the world's top women billionaires, four times more than the US, Hurun research institute reveals', *South China Morning Post*, 27 March 2021

surveyed were stressed from work, which was higher than the global average of 84 per cent.[7] The survey also highlights that Singaporean women experienced more unmanageable stress at work, which lead them to neglect their physical health more than men.

From all accounts, the tendency to work hard seems to be more pronounced for women. It is common to hear women speak of work in terms of time spent on the job, including weekends. As an experienced leader puts it, 'I think the whole idea of self-identity for the Singaporean woman is perhaps less evolved. Who you are is defined by your title and your job.'

As per Grant Thornton's Women in Business 2022 report[8] the proportion of Singapore mid-market businesses with at least one woman in senior management has gone up to 92 per cent, up from 90 per cent. The most common leadership roles that women hold are human resources director and chief finance officer (CFO), coming in at 49 per cent and 43 per cent, respectively.

Another finding is that globally, 24 per cent of mid-market businesses have female chief executive officers (CEOs) or managing directors (MDs). This figure for Southeast Asia stands at 32 per cent. However, the proportion of mid-market businesses in Singapore with CEOs and MDs is relatively much lower at 11 per cent.

'Safe and serious' may be a good way to describe both Singapore and its women. Women often project a combination

---

[7] Neo Rong Wei, 'Sleep-deprived Singaporean workers among most stressed globally: Survey, *Today* 26 March, 2019, (www.todayonline.com)

[8] Women in Business 2022 Report, Grant Thornton, Singapore 2022

of seriousness, competence and conservatism. Much like the city-state, they are reliable, practical and efficient.

When one takes into consideration the manner in which women dress for work, there is a sense that, in general, the clothes and shoes they wear are template, safe and similar. Their clothes aren't flamboyant or loud in their choice of style or colours. In a sense, they are a reflection of the deeper nuances of conformity and staidness. As Karen Tay Koh, independent non-executive director on the boards of several companies in Singapore, observes: 'Women leaders in Singapore have a tendency to stay within a safe space. There's a strong sense of 'don't rock the boat too much and don't offend people'. However entrepreneurial female leaders, who are young and dynamic, might think differently.

Thailand

According to Thai tradition, women are often compared to the 'hind legs' of an elephant while the men are the 'front legs'. While this could be inferred as men lead and women follow,[9] it should be noted that Thai women have made significant progress in the corporate world.

Thailand, a country that has much respect for traditions, is one of the more liberal and tolerant places in Southeast Asia. Thailand scores 34 on Hofstede's feminine dimension and is thus considered a feminine society. A feminine society is one with less assertiveness and competitiveness, where the dominant values are caring for others and quality of life.

---

9 Astrid S. Tuminez, Rising to The Top – A Report on Women's Leadership in Asia, Lee Kuan Yew School of Public Policy, National University of Singapore, 2012

From all accounts, Thai women consider themselves to be equal to men and don't feel the need to seek special privileges. Perhaps a case in point is the manner in which International Women's Day is celebrated in Thailand. In neighbouring countries such as Vietnam, it is customary for male colleagues to give a rose to their female colleagues; practices such as this are not the norm in Thailand. According to a senior HR director of a multinational corporation, 'Working in Thailand is quite fair and more performance-driven rather than gender-driven. In our organization, we have 70 per cent of our workforce as female employees so I would say that if anything it might be the men who feel that they are the minority in the organization!'

Thai women are a step ahead in terms of personal gratification. As Beiersdorf's ASEAN[10] senior vice president, Rakshit Hargave had a ringside view of the personal care products industry. His observation was that Thai women are conscious of their skin and overall personality, and they take the lead in spending and taking care of themselves.

Thai women make up more than one-third of senior management positions, and many have inherited family businesses. As per Grant Thornton's Women in Business 2021 Report for Thailand, women held 29 per cent of senior management positions in mid-size businesses in Thailand.[11] Notwithstanding this data point, Thai women are successful in the corporate world.

On reason for this is the Thai family structure, which allows one to live with parents and grandparents, enables women to

---

10 Association of Southeast Asian Nations, comprising ten member countries

11 Women in Business 2021 Report, Grant Thornton, Thailand 2021

continue to work. Another factor that helps is the availability and affordability of domestic help.

Interestingly, in Thailand, while there are many women leaders in the corporate world, there are fewer in politics. For a range of reasons, women may prefer to work in the corporate world than in politics.

Japan

Given the importance of harmony or '*wa*' in Japanese society, conformity and perfection are greatly valued. This drive for excellence and perfection is evident in all walks of life. I have always been struck by the emphasis and care the Japanese give to creating the perfect external appearance whether it pertains to a cake, a gift or a person.

However, there is often a dissonance between the seemingly perfect external façade or behaviour and the underlying reality. Over coffee in a Singapore café, Yurika Kurakata, who works in professional development on East Asia for educators in the United States, shared how one of the first things many children in Japan are taught is not to cry in public places, as it disturbs people! Clearly, being mindful of others starts young. On a related note, filial duty and family responsibilities often override personal success or happiness.

Other values that are prevalent are the ingrained obedience, the reluctance to question authority, group-ism and insularity.[12] As Yurika points out, in general the work culture in Japan has

---

[12] 'Lessons in Leadership from the Fukushima Nuclear Disaster,' *Knowledge at Wharton*, 3 October 2013, https://knowledge.wharton.upenn.edu/article/lessons-leadership-fukushima-nuclear-disaster/

been less about grooming leaders and leaders-to-be and more about fostering followers who will listen and cooperate without questioning or challenging. This is gradually changing, but slowly.

Working long hours is the norm in Japan. And because death by overwork is not uncommon, they even have a word for it: *karoshi*, which refers to employees dying from stress-related ailments or to people taking their lives because of the pressures of the job. The propensity to work long hours doesn't make it easier for women managers and leaders.

If Thailand and the Philippines are on the progressive end of the scale, more east literally and figuratively is Japan. In 2012, late Prime Minister Shinzo Abe rolled out 'Womenomics', a policy thrust aimed to help women 'shine'. However, these policies do not seem to have significantly moved the needle with regard to ingrained mindsets and women's empowerment in Japan.

In 2022, Japan ranked 116th amongst 146 countries in the gender gap rankings index of the World Economic Forum (WEF), taking the last spot amongst the Group of Seven industrialized nations. On a related note, despite 72 per cent of Japanese women being in the labour force, women are employed in just 14.7 per cent of senior roles.[13]

India

On a recent trip to Mumbai, a hoarding on a small hardware shop caught my eye. On the red-coloured hoarding, typed in prominent white letters were the words 'RV & Daughters'. I did a double take because these signs usually have the words '&

---

13 'Japan ranks 120th in 2021 gender gap report, worst among G-7,' Kyodo News, 31 March 2021

Sons' almost like a suffix, indicative of the practice wherein sons take over shops, companies and family businesses. Increasingly, however, there is a trend of more daughters taking over family businesses and running them well.

A paradox on many levels, India is chaotic and unpredictable but also vibrant and dynamic. It is a society where hierarchy and relationships coexist, as do collectivist and individualist traits. It is a place where time is relatively fluid, yet everything is needed 'at the earliest'.

This dichotomy is prevalent throughout. At one level, society is patriarchal and at another, India has had both a woman prime minister and woman president. While women face many biases and challenges, they have done particularly well in fields such as banking and information technology, with many women assuming leadership positions in banks and financial institutions.

Historically, women in Indian society have been seen as nurturers and providers while men were the deciders or the breadwinners in the family. While this is changing, women are largely expected to bear the lion's share of the obligations at home.

India ranks third in the world for women in senior management positions in mid-size businesses, according to Grant Thornton's Women in Business 2021 Report. The percentage of women in senior management for India stood at 39 per cent, as against the global average of 31 per cent, which may be reflective of the changing outlook of Indian businesses towards working women.[14]

---

14 'India ranks third in the world for women working in senior management positions: Report', ETHRWorld, 3 March 2021, https://hr.economictimes.indiatimes.com/news/workplace-4-0/diversity-and-inclusion/india-ranks-third-in-the-worl

Where the opportunities are provided and the environment is conducive, women have done well, be it a village, a tier-two city or a bustling metro. That said, the journey for women is less linear and more nuanced, much like everything else in India.

The landscape: facts and figures

Grant Thornton's Women in Business 2022 Report provides an overview of the representation of women in senior management around the world. As per this report, 32 per cent of senior positions in mid-market businesses around the world are now held by women. Also 90 per cent of businesses report having at least one woman in their senior management team.[15]

When the '30 per cent' number of women in senior roles globally was reached in 2021, it was considered to be an important milestone that would catalyze gender diversity. However as can be seen, there hasn't been a significant increase in this figure in 2022.

The report indicates variations across different regions. Africa has the highest representation with 40 per cent of senior roles being held by women leaders. ASEAN is the second highest performer at 37 per cent. Interestingly, ASEAN which constitutes emerging markets like Indonesia, Malaysia and Thailand seems to be doing better than Asia-Pacific (APAC) where the representation is at 30 per cent. One reason for this could be that APAC includes countries such as Japan that lag behind on this metric.

This was also seen in 2021, as per the illustration below.

---

15 Women in Business Report, Grant Thornton International, 2022

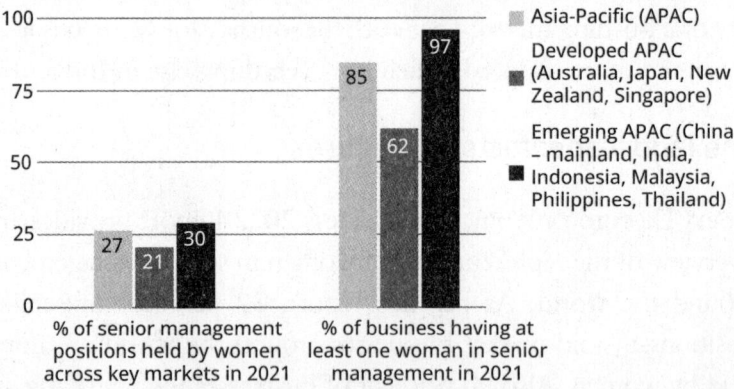

Source: Data from Grant Thornton's Women in Business 2021 Report

In 2022, while the overall figure of women's representation in senior roles stands at 32 per cent globally, only 24 per cent of women are CEOs/MDs. APAC lags behind at 16 per cent whereas ASEAN is at 32 per cent.

With regard to the roles, the role of CFO has the highest female representation. More than half (53 per cent) of CFO positions in ASEAN are held by women. The interplay between culture and gender partially explains the large number of women CFOs in the region. In Thai and Chinese culture, money has traditionally been the woman's domain.[16] Although India is not a part of ASEAN, it is relevant to mention that many women have reached the top echelons of the banking and finance sector.

---

16 Watanan Petersik, 'Beyond the Glass Ceiling,' in Astrid S. Tuminez and Maria del Mar Garza (eds.), *Women Leaders and the New Asian Century*, 2014

Asian economies have made huge strides in the past few decades. They have achieved significant economic growth and progressed on areas like health, education and employment. In Asia, many women caregivers and domestic helpers are the primary breadwinners.

Overall, as seen from the data above, there is progress in the numbers in women's leadership. But this progress is nuanced across the region and there is a gender gap in the top rungs of leadership. Also from all accounts, women's representation in the public sector and politics in Asia lags behind.

On a big picture level, some aberrations and contrasts are observed. One observation is that economic development does not necessarily translate to increased women's leadership. A few advanced economies like Japan and South Korea perform poorly in some measures of women's leadership such as women in senior management, women on boards, remuneration and political empowerment.[17] Another dichotomy is that the countries of South Asia which lag behind on gender equality lead the way in political empowerment. These countries have had several women heads of state. However, this is primarily on account of family and dynastic connections and cannot be attributed to greater gender equality.

Women on boards

A recent report by Deloitte on women in the boardroom found that in 2021, women hold just 19.7 per cent of board seats globally.

---

[17] Astrid S. Tuminez, Rising to The Top – A Report on Women's Leadership in Asia, Lee Kuan Yew School of Public Policy, National University of Singapore, 2012

In terms of the countries in Southeast Asia, the countries of Indonesia, Malaysia, the Philippines, Singapore, Thailand and Vietnam have collectively fared better with an average of 17.1 per cent of women in board seats. This outperforms the Asia average of 11.7 per cent.[18]

Board seats held by women

Countries	Percentage of board seats held by women
China	13.1
Singapore	17.6
Malaysia	24
Philippines	17.7
India	17.1
Indonesia	8.3
Japan	8.2
Thailand	17.8
Australia	29.6
New Zealand	31.9
USA	23.9
UK	30.1
France	43.2

Source: Women in the Boardroom: A Global Perspective, Deloitte, published in February 2022

---

18 Deloitte Women in the Boardroom Report Press Release https://www2.deloitte.com/sg/en/pages/cxo-programs/articles/deloitte-women-in-the-boardroom-report-press-release.html

These findings indicate a significant variance in women's participation in boards across geographies.

With regards to CEO roles held by women, Singapore (13.1 per cent) and Thailand (11.6 per cent) are ranked first and third respectively among the countries surveyed. It may be relevant to point out that India was one of the first emerging markets to mandate a gender quota on corporate boards. In 2013 the Companies Act mandated that all publicly listed firms should have at least one-woman director.

What's culture got to do with it?

On a big picture level, when one looks at Southeast Asia, there are a large number of women in the workforce. As a leader shared with me, 'Honestly, ASEAN was very used to (having) senior women leaders. So it was not a big deal for me when I became one.' Many offices, especially in places like Singapore, are fairly diverse both from a culture and gender standpoint. In countries such as Thailand and Philippines, the working population is skewed with a sizeable number of working women, who are often the 'stable ship' of the house. However, the picture is different in countries like Japan and India, where there are comparatively fewer women in senior management.

One reason for the progress in ASEAN is changing mindsets and attitudes towards female leaders.[19] But the progress is nuanced. While Southeast Asia seems to be faring well, the reality is that only a very small percentage of these women become CEOs or MDs, compared to their male counterparts.

Culture, often perceived as an intangible concept not being relevant to professional growth, impacts women's success.

---

19 Women in Business Report, Grant Thornton International, 2022

Deep-rooted perceptions of gender roles, traditional beliefs and stereotypes impact how women work and lead at different stages in their career. Also, in research conducted by the World Economic Forum of women from 600 companies in twenty BRIC and OECD countries, the respondents cited 'their country's general norms and cultural practices' as one of the top three barriers to women's rise to leadership.[20]

'Asian women aren't unique from women in the West, but their challenges are a bit more unique.' This is an observation of a senior leader who works in both the West and Asia. Senela Jayasuriya, founder of Women Empowered Global who also works across both worlds, puts this in context: 'In both the West and Asia, there are intersectional and systemic challenges that career women face. However, in the Asian context, more specifically in South Asia, a prevalent challenge is the generational mindset associated with gender roles at home and at the workplace.'

It is important to note that in the past two years, the Covid-19 pandemic impacted people's careers and lives in different ways. While the pandemic enabled everyone to balance their professional and personal lives, women have borne the brunt in terms of increased household responsibilities and reduced job prospects. This is particularly true in parts of Asia.

---

20 Astrid S. Tuminez, Rising to The Top – A Report on Women's Leadership in Asia, Lee Kuan Yew School of Public Policy, National University of Singapore, 2012

Conclusion

There are several factors that impact careers. Culture is not tangible or quantifiable and, in many cases, its impact is not directly evident. However cultural factors often play a larger role than they are given credit for. We will discuss in the pages ahead how cultural norms impact the way credibility is perceived, confidence is manifested, and ambition is expressed.

In this chapter, I have outlined some cultural values and nuances in a few countries in Asia and their impact on work and life. This provides a context and basis for the rest of the book. Given that these values are prevalent throughout Asia, both men and women have learnt to conform to and work around them. But since the focus is on women leaders in this book, we will explore in the next chapters how women work around these aspects to rise and dazzle.

2

Courage and Control

Shashi Iyer,[21] head of the India business of a large US multinational, was in an annual leadership review meeting. In the discussion on future growth of the 'top twenty talents' in his country office, his American boss felt that the local vice president (VP) didn't have the necessary assertiveness and persona to be promoted to the next level. Although the VP brought in the numbers and managed the team well, his leadership style was perceived as being different and 'Eastern'.

This oversimplification or categorization of leadership is not uncommon. Much of leadership across Asia is characterized by an understated, less flamboyant and less vocal style, which is often labelled as 'Asian' leadership. Those who are not familiar with the cultural nuances may attribute the apparent lack of assertiveness or speaking up to a dearth of confidence or drive. In reality, these behaviours are often driven by underlying values

---

21 Pseudonym

of humility, respect and the need to maintain harmony and be in sync with the power structures and group dynamics.

Bonita Lee, a senior leader, emerging markets, at a multinational company explains it thus:

> If you work within an Asian context, it may feel like more details are needed to support actions; where the confidence to move forward is not as clear. This may come from having to make sure that everything is near perfect before going forward. The fear of failure is more prevalent here versus in Western cultures, although the younger generation may be better able to take risks.

At the risk of stereotyping, she puts in perspective the broad nuances of how confidence and control play out in this part of the world. In cases where more data is needed to support actions, there may be a more cautious approach, and the confidence to move forward is not expressed overtly.

Let's consider Singapore, where a huge premium is placed on perfection and accuracy. A recent example that comes to mind is the manner of managing people at the designated centres for Covid vaccines. The flow and movement of people from the time they entered the makeshift centre to checking their details, getting the vaccine, and subsequently waiting for thirty minutes was driven by a meticulous systems approach. This planning and precision, down to the smallest detail, drives the way everything is done in Singapore. The corollary of this approach is the need for more data to support actions in order to minimize mistakes and failures, often accentuated by the educational emphasis on getting things right.

It's relevant to mention here that the nuance of 'kiasu' aids and abets this thinking and behaviour. *Kiasu* is a Hokkien (Chinese dialect) word that comes from *kia*, meaning afraid, and *su*, meaning to lose, which adds up to the fear of losing out.[22] In 2007 the word was included in the Oxford English Dictionary, where it is defined as a person 'governed by self-interest, typically manifesting as a selfish, grasping attitude arising from a fear of missing out on something.' Both a noun and an adjective, *kiasu* is rooted in the need for a small nation to be self-reliant, competitive and stay ahead. This gets manifested in a fear of losing out, whether it's in a queue for the latest phone or admission into a coveted school.

In Singapore, given the societal reliance on data and the need for 100 per cent accuracy, there is a tendency for managers to check and double-check that everything is perfect before going forward. And while these tendencies hold true across the board, they seem to be more pronounced in the way women work and lead in Singapore. On a related note, the tendency for women leaders to be more uptight and less open in sharing information is possibly a defence mechanism in a male-dominated work environment.

Another factor contributing to the focus on 'getting it right' could be the tiger mom factor. Tiger mom or *hu ma* is a Mandarin phrase, which refers to a strict, protective mother who pushes her children to be the very best in academics and other fields. In some cases, leaders are seen to bring their tiger mom side to work when they act determined and competitive. As one leader puts it, 'You don't just have to pass an exam with A's, you also need to get your A's at work.'

Speaking of details and data, here is how Chris Ng, senior business leader of an organization in Singapore, works with her team.

---

22 Sarah Keating, 'The most ambitious country in the world?' BBC Travel, 13 March 2018

How Chris leads

One aspect of my way of working is that I get into understanding the details, yet retain a high-level perspective to drive decisions and actions. My finance background helps me work better with data, and I use it to build a business case.

I operate with the 80-20 rule; I don't need 100 per cent accuracy. If the data is fine at 80 per cent accuracy and confidence level, my approach is to work with it to get things done. If one focuses too much on the facts being correct, the opportunity would be lost.

Once my team understands the deliverables, I don't get into how they do it; they are capable enough! I don't micromanage because who wants to work for a micromanager? In my team, we have open communication. I want people to tell me as it is. If something is not right, we work on fixing it together.

In my experience, male leaders operate from a high level, seldom delving into the details. On the other hand, women usually prefer to just deal with the details. They don't want to be talking about the big picture because they are worried 'what if I say something wrong?'

But when women make a conscious choice to manage details while also being comfortable enough to speak up at a big picture level, then it's a different story! These are women who can lead successfully. Women should know when to be detail-oriented and when to zoom out and be more strategic and macro.

> Chris recognizes that in order to be agile and respond to business opportunities, an over-reliance on the facts being 100 per cent correct isn't always prudent. Focusing on details is a good quality to have, but the ability to zoom out to see the bigger picture and strategize is equally important.

A few leaders shared how they consciously devised a more hands-off leadership style in their organizations. They encourage their teams to not get bogged down by the details and to find new ways to think outside the box. Greater flexibility and less control help unleash creativity and empower employees. The devil isn't always in the details!

Collaboration

If control lies at one end of the spectrum, where would collaboration be placed?

> I found it interesting that almost every woman leader I spoke with, across different countries, industries and roles, used the word 'collaborative' as one of the first few words to describe herself. It made me wonder: was this a 'nice to have' or a 'need to have' attribute?
>
> In general, women may be keener to build consensus, probably because of the innate desire to please, which is prevalent in this part of the world. As Jon E. Kaplan, an American who spent several years in Asia, says, 'The desire to meet and exceed expectations is stronger amidst Asian women.'

In this chapter, we explore how leaders leverage their collaborative approach in a grounded and practical way. One such leader is Lynette V. Ortiz, the CEO of Standard Chartered Bank in the Philippines. She has worked in New York and Singapore on international assignments. In this account, Lynette highlights her style of leading and working.

How Lynette leads

My leadership style is inclusive and collaborative. I listen, but as a person and a leader I am decisive because the buck has to stop somewhere. After you get the inputs from everybody, a decision has to be made and someone has to be accountable; I step up to that.

One of the many challenges I have faced and continue to do so is managing a large, diverse team that will buy into the strategy, embrace it and execute it with enthusiasm and energy. The first step is for people to understand and embrace that the strategy and purpose make sense and resonate with them. As a leader, one has to provide a balance of autonomy and oversight, giving people room to execute. Another challenge as a leader is to make the tough decisions around having the right team members and coming to decisions around how some are not the right fit.

This entails investing time to communicate and listen. Listening is not easy because as a leader there is a tendency to be prescriptive. I had a senior leader sharing with us insights around how one has to know when to be in the balcony and when to be on the dance floor—excellent advice, which I take to heart.

As a leader, you always want to paint yourself in a good way and build hope and optimism, but you need to be able to look back and assess what worked and didn't. Oftentimes, leaders feel that it's an aspersion on their character if they have to course correct, but admitting mistakes is important. If there are mistakes in decisions, as there will be, accepting these is important.

As one of two women leaders in the banking sector in the country, Lynette is tenacious and driven. An intuitive leader, she knows how to leverage the power of relationships to drive outcomes successfully. Lynette steps up to being accountable for her actions and takes ownership of them. She accepts her mistakes and is willing to course correct, when needed.

Lynette makes a good point about listening, something that is not obvious and is often overlooked, even at senior levels! As Senela Jayasuriya, keynote speaker and empowerment coach, says, 'If we want buy-in, it's important to first listen to what the other person is saying. We have our narrative and objective, but you really have to be open to the other person's first and then express what we mean.'.

Roshni Nadar Malhotra, chairperson of HCL Tech, India, is another example of a leader who has a collaborative style. Whether it's with her colleagues at HCL Tech or externally, Roshni likes to take people along. She describes herself as a 'collaborative but a decisive leader'.

> When they have the big picture in mind, these women leaders create a collaborative process, where it's back and forth rather than strictly top-down. They seek to break silos and are able to make connections between different teams.
>
> Collaborative leaders may be perceived as not being decisive, something that both Lynette and Roshni seem to be cognizant of.
>
> And while having a collaborative style is great, one has to know where to draw the line. Chloe, (not her real name) a leader in China, puts it well: 'I have a tendency to keep my door open. I make decisions after reviewing them with the team. However, in order to enable employees to take responsibility and to find solutions on their own, I have learnt to close the door sometimes.'

In their well-articulated piece on collaborative leadership,[23] Kathryn Heath, Jill Flynn and Mary Davis Holt point out that 'The best collaborative leaders are able to maintain their executive presence: They articulate a vision, provide inspiration and then give their teams enough latitude to creatively and effectively work toward a defined end that suits the organization.'

Providing this latitude requires leaders to be comfortable with dissent and diversity, a quality that Vanitha Narayanan has inculcated, as she shares:

> When I look at being effective, I have never been intimidated by having people on my team that are smarter than me. If you have a team that looks at things just like you, you are going to have a collective blind spot. If you have a team that thinks differently and challenges you, you are better prepared when you step into the marketplace.
>
> But this requires you to be comfortable with not having complete agreement all the time because as women, we often seek consensus, but you are not going to move things at a fast enough pace if you always wait for consensus. Being collaborative can appear to be indecisive so while you seek out strong and diverse views and voices, you have got to be decisive and move on.

Vanitha Narayanan, former managing director and chairman, IBM India, is secure in the face of different viewpoints and opinions, which is not a common quality amongst leaders, especially those in hierarchical cultures, who are often unused to, or uncomfortable with, dissent or disagreement. Vanitha's approach is refreshing and is reflective of a new approach in the 'new normal' world we live in.

---

23 Kathryn Heath, Jill Flynn and Mary Davis Holt, 'The Upside and Downside of Collaborative Leadership', in the HBR *Guide for Women at Work*, Harvard Business Review Press, 2019

WHAT'S IN HER BAG: TRICKS OR TRAITS

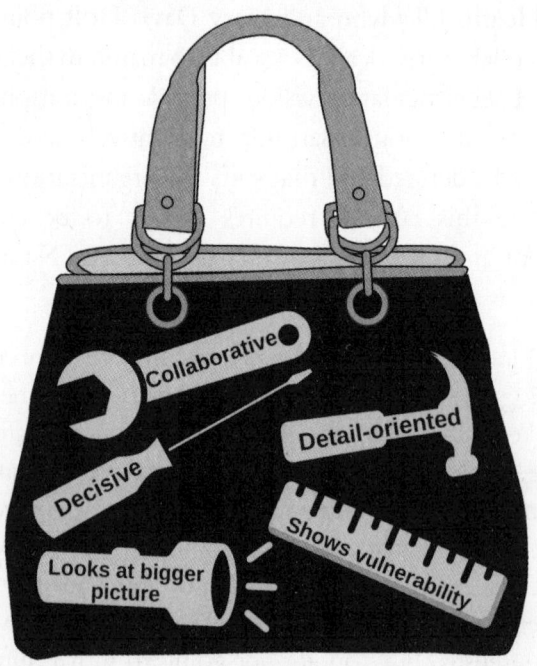

Open and approachable

A related attribute of leaders who are secure is that of being open and transparent. This is something Dr Harpreet A. De Singh, executive director of Air India, epitomizes as she elaborates further:

> My office is an open office, anyone can walk in with a suggestion, a comment or criticism. As a leader, I have told my team numerous times to feel free to tell me if I'm wrong or if I have overlooked something.
> One has to connect with people; you have to break these barriers of senior, middle and frontline levels in an organization. The middle level in an organization plays an important role since they know what's happening at the frontline, and they

also know what senior management wants. But often, they hold on to information and are reluctant to escalate. If the middle management is not motivated enough to do the right thing, they can be the biggest stumbling block.

I address the entire airline online and go to meet the frontline staff and ask them to share the issues they face. And I then encourage the middle management to bridge the gap.

I believe in transparency and don't think of myself as a CEO. The moment you go on that ego trip, people don't open up. I am not attached to the chair.

It is evident that Harpreet believes less in hierarchy and more in being approachable. She has her finger on the pulse of the organization and is tuned in to how people think and feel.

Women leaders, by and large, are perceived to be approachable. Also, they are perceptibly less bogged down by hierarchy and its trappings. As a male leader observes, 'Women leaders tend to treat you more as an equal, despite the hierarchy.'

Courage and vulnerability

When Nayantara Bali took up her first board assignment with a Singaporean company in the technology sector, she was very aware that 'she did not understand' a few technicalities. Nayantara, director of ANV Consulting Pte, and independent director of a few publicly listed companies in Singapore, India and the UK, shares this candid account of her experience:

When I came on board, I had to get up to speed quickly. As a non-technical person, I was unfamiliar with the wheels of the business. So, in the first couple of meetings, I was working hard to understand the nitty-gritty of the telecom sector. Since many of the terms and acronyms were unfamiliar, I requested a 'ready reckoner' that would be handy. My request led to them organizing a half-day knowledge session.

Interestingly, this was insightful for everybody, not just the newer directors, as the pace of technology in the sector was so fast that it helped all keep pace with the latest. At the time, I had felt hesitant to ask for a knowledge-sharing session, but I was glad that it benefited everyone. My learning was: you should ask for help and not worry about how you may be perceived when you don't know enough because as a director, it's your job to understand the dynamics of the industry.

How often do we see managers and leaders seeking more clarity, especially in a new role or an unfamiliar setting? Doing so as a woman is perhaps more uncommon, which is why Nayantara's example is real and commendable.

On a related note, Chris narrates how she approaches situations where she doesn't know the answer. If she doesn't understand something, she seeks a clarification from her boss, saying, 'Boss, I need to ask you a silly question'. By labelling it as 'silly', she underplays it, making him or her more receptive to her query. As she says, it's better than calling the question 'stupid', a word she's banned her kids from using!

What stood out for me about this anecdote was that Chris doesn't take herself too seriously. She is fine to admit that she doesn't know something and in fact goes a step further by prefacing her question as 'silly'.

> The above anecdotes illustrate how being open and asking for clarity is an indication of how secure leaders display their discomfort or lack of familiarity with a topic. Saying 'I don't understand' or 'I don't know' is difficult for leaders, especially in cultures where they are placed on a pedestal and expected to dispense solutions. But leaders who are comfortable expressing this come across as transparent and courageous, qualities that have resonated during recent times.

Speaking of courage, women leaders do dare to do things differently. They do step beyond what is asked or needed; they are not afraid to go outside the lines. When needed, they facilitate change and disruption. Sunsanee Supatravanij, independent director of a Thai listed company and mentor to health tech start-ups, highlights how she enables and embraces change:

> Sometimes one needs to make changes to structures, processes and the composition of teams. This disrupts things as people don't want to move out of their comfort zone, but if there are impediments to how the team works and delivers, changes need to be made, and this is where, as a leader, you have to dare to make those changes. My role is to unlock their ideas and contribution so that the organization can move forward.

The definition of courageous leadership has evolved, and as the above instances show, courage is no longer about being the toughest or the loudest in a room. In the essay, 'What courageous leaders do differently',[24] James R. Detert points out that once people know one is competent, it makes you look strong (not weak) when you admit that you don't know something or say 'please help with this'.

An example of this approach is shared by Pavitra Singh. A few months after Pavitra took over as chief human resources officer (CHRO) of PepsiCo India in October 2019, the pandemic struck. Like other leaders navigating an unfamiliar situation, she wasn't sure how to manage, but showing her vulnerability helped her to be more receptive to people's opinions. Being open and admitting that she didn't know everything helped Pavitra build a common understanding and trust. She felt that showing her

---

24 James R. Detert, 'What courageous leaders do differently,' *Harvard Business Review*, 7 January 2022

vulnerability allowed people to partner with her to work with the best ideas and make better decisions because 'everyone was in it together'.

> Research indicates that leaders who openly accept mistakes are seen as more trustworthy and likeable as compared to those who deflect criticism and cover up their mistakes. However, while showing one's vulnerability is an indication of being secure, it may not work in all situations. There is a time and place to show vulnerability—especially as a female leader.

Abanti Sankaranarayanan, chief public affairs officer, Mahindra Group, India, puts the above in perspective:

> It's okay to show both strength and vulnerability, but you have to show them at the right time, in the right context. In a crisis, you can be open to listening and draw more people in to find the solution while leading with strength, not vulnerability.
>
> Showing your vulnerability is a huge strength because only if you are very self-assured and secure will you show it! However, as a woman leader in India, you've got to be careful because the conventional perception in India of a strong leader is (that) you are a superhero who knows everything, is supremely confident and has never failed. When as a woman you show vulnerability, people are often very quick to say it's your gender that is causing you to be vulnerable. And that undermines your innate role as a leader, which is what you want to be seen as and not as a 'woman leader'.
>
> So you've got to be a little more careful about when, where and to what extent you show vulnerability, and the culture of the organization plays a big role.

Abanti raises a valid point that vulnerability can be a strength, provided it is manifested at the right time and place. In the Indian context, leaders are expected to have the knowledge, the experience and the answers. Therefore, admitting one doesn't know the answers may not always be a good idea; the context should be conducive for this to be taken in the intended spirit.

Humility

Much has been said about how the women leading countries such as New Zealand, Taiwan, Iceland, Finland, Norway and Germany during the pandemic managed to keep cases and deaths in control. They followed rules, relied on experts and were transparent in sharing their rationale and actions with their people. As author C.Y. Gopinath writes in an article, these women led the way 'with a little humility, a little warmth and a little science'.[25]

At the risk of generalizing, that seems to be the formula for success in Asia—crisis or no crisis! As discussed earlier, humility is an important value in much of Asia. To give an example, Filipinos are innately humble. There is an old Filipino proverb that says, 'He who does not know how to look back at where he came from will never reach his destination.' Humility is a value that is ingrained amongst most Thais. It is also an important trait for the Chinese; as a Chinese person described, women prefer to hide their value instead of expressing it.

Humility enables people to accept and acknowledge mistakes and be more open and tolerant leaders. However, as pointed out

---

25 C.Y. Gopinath, 'When women lead, the virus loses', *Mid-day*, 9 June 2020, https://www.mid-day.com/news/opinion/article/When-women-lead--the-virus-loses-22833266

in a *Harvard Business Review* article,[26] humility is often seen as a feminine trait, which must change, as it is a critical driver of leadership effectiveness in both men and women.

As discussed, women leaders are able to balance seemingly contrary nuances such as strength and humility. The anecdotes below show yet again how they balance varied aspects such as global and local expectations.

Bridging global and local

A challenge that many business leaders grapple with is striving to keep the balance between global and local. In this context, let's consider Anna's challenges as she works with her global leaders. Anna Cortes,[27] CEO of a large multinational corporation (MNC) in the Philippines, shares:

> Since we support global clients and my employees are Filipinos, I often feel that there is a disconnect between global expectations and Filipino traits. For instance, humility is a much-valued trait in the Philippines. If people tell you 'You are so senior and yet so humble' it's a compliment! But in a global setting where you are supposed to be assertive and confident, that's not necessarily a compliment. So, maintaining this balance is a unique challenge—I have to make sure that I support my global clients and develop my Filipino colleagues to be global leaders while harnessing their strengths.
>
> Another unique aspect is harnessing the Filipino pride. People rally around their heroes; for example, when the renowned Filipino boxer Manny Pacquiao has a fight, it's a big

---

26 Tomas Chamorro Premuzic and Cindy Gallop, '7 Leadership Lessons Men Can Learn from Women', *Harvard Business Review*, 1 April 2020

27 Name changed to protect identity

deal in the Philippines! So, every time we craft our strategy or vision, I make it a point to display Filipino talent. For example, our strategy to be the destination of choice for our clients was centred on the amazing Filipino creativity; when we showcase this, it always evokes an emotional response from my team.

As the CEO of an MNC in the Philippines, Anna has to reconcile the priorities and interests of different teams and stakeholders. She leverages the passion and pride her Filipino colleagues have by making an emotional connect to their work.

In a similar vein, Adele Tao Leader of LIXIL Water Technology in China shares her predicament of reconciling different nuances in a global world, a challenge commonly experienced by leaders.

The culture of China is about hierarchy, but multinational companies have a strong mindset of democracy. So, when I work with my team, I combine both these nuances and try to balance them. The hierarchy helps to make sure everything is on track to move forward. But before we take the final decision, we have a lot of discussions. I try and make sure everyone speaks up—from my leadership team to the people in junior roles. So, we respect the hierarchy but democracy helps us make sure we include different voices and perspectives in order to reduce risks and succeed.

As to how my team balances global MNC expectations with local concerns and resources, we first consider what takes priority, global or local? We assess what customers and other business partners in each of their markets expect. Will local strategy turn out to be more successful or vice versa?

Often, they cannot replicate the strategy, approach or practices that originate from the global head office. Based on the directions that originate from the head office, the team develops their strategy and plans for China. But in the absence of known practices or examples, we work with the team to figure out what is the optimal solution to adopt. They recognize and leverage their organizational capabilities and collaborate across borders, as needed.

> As the head of an MNC in China, Adele shares how she leverages the best of both worlds. In a 'boss-driven' culture, it takes time for colleagues to share views and bring new ideas instead of following them. An Asian leader who was based in China says how it was normal for her to hear her colleagues concur with her saying 'whatever you say' or 'of course'. In the anecdote above, Adele highlights how she encourages a more inclusive style of working within the hierarchical structure.
>
> We saw how in the earlier example, as CEO of a MNC in the Philippines, Anna reconciles priorities and interests of different teams and stakeholders. These challenges such as managing global and local expectations and interests are commonly experienced by country leaders of MNCs; however, they are not always called out by leaders or taken into consideration by their colleagues in other markets.

In conclusion, Lani Darmawan, a senior Indonesian leader says it well: 'If society and men think that women are softer, understanding and listen more, yes, we are like that. But it goes back to our confidence—do we see it as a positive or as a weakness? The way I see it, it's a strength.'

Being courageous and vulnerable are not contradictory. These leaders stand tall yet sway gracefully and bend over in humility.

They said

- There is a tendency to compare one's success with that of their batchmates. Often, this comparison with one's undergrad batchmates or business school batchmates goes on for many years. This view of ambition is very unidimensional and can be self-limiting. Women who are secure and can move beyond this, do well.' – Dr Rohini Srivathsa
- Success is having the clarity of desiring something and having the muscle power to achieve it and the power to overcome. Those are the two things where a lot of people fail. They want success but the roadmap is difficult because they don't have clarity in their desire, nor do they have the muscle power to achieve it.
- I want young, aspiring women leaders to learn from what the earlier leaders have gone through and to be strategic in the way they manage their career. I feel that a lot of women don't think it through in being strategic.

3

Results and Relationships

Polly Ng is the CEO of Global Women Connect, a social enterprise, and president and CEO of BWS Group, (Aquaculture AI Solutions). Originally from Hong Kong, she was based in China in global and regional leadership positions. She shares one of her experiences and learnings:

> During my initial days of working in China, I had an aggressive, fast-paced style of working, a style that is common to leaders from Hong Kong. I was driven, direct and very result-oriented, but I quickly realized that this style didn't work. My team was stressed, and their performance dropped; they wanted me to be less demanding and talk of things other than work.
>
> I realized that working in China is a bit different as 'guanxi' is important. So a leader in China needs to balance both relationships and goals. I had to change my style of working and leading the team. Instead of being only focused

on results, I tried to connect more with people. I continued to push myself but stopped pushing the team as much. They appreciated that I gave them some space and let them do things their way. Eventually, they picked up the pace and took more initiative.

> Polly's observation highlights that while hierarchy is an important dynamic, so is fostering trust and building relationships. This is similar to Arisa's experience in Thailand, discussed earlier. While Polly was familiar with working in the region, she realized that she the needed to adapt her leadership style in order to be more effective in China.
>
> Polly's experience is not an isolated one. A European director on the board of a Chinese company remarked how she was surprised by the need to meet and create relationships in China outside of board meetings. She found this a bit different compared to other places that she had lived in or was familiar with.
>
> In much of Asia, it's about managing and balancing the task and the team. However, the nuances of building relationships and forging ties differ across countries.

In China, managers and leaders need to be cognizant of building relationships or *guanxi* with employees, business partners and suppliers, government officials and customers.

In the book *China CEO: Voices of Experience from 20 International Business Leaders* by Juan Antonio Fernandez and Laurie Underwood,[28] *guanxi* is defined as a gateway or connection

---

28 Juan Antonio Fernandez and Laurie Underwood, John Wiley & Sons (Asia) Pte Ltd, Singapore 2006

between two people created by a link of mutual obligation to each other. In Mandarin, *guan* means 'gate' and *xi* means 'links'. While it exists between families, classmates and acquaintances, one is referring to business *guanxi* in the context of working in China. In a sense, *guanxi* serves as a form of social currency with both sides keeping track of favours given and favours owed, a concept which is far stronger in China.

> ### Women Leaders in China: A Perspective
>
> Mike Liu, former managing director for DXC Technology Greater China, describes successful women leaders in China as those who have clear objectives in both short term and medium term, delivering results and earning the trust of senior leaders. They are not easily influenced by biased views or distractions. In short, they are focused, result-oriented and work hard to build relationships and trust.

While on the subject of fostering relationships, let's discuss how this works in the Philippines.

The art of 'malasakit'

Lucy was asked by her global CEO, 'What do you mean by *malasakit*? I hear this term often when working with Filipinos.'

Lucy,[29] a senior leader at a call centre based in Manila, was in conversation with her CEO and went on to explain that *malasakit* is a Filipino trait, which means having a personal investment in the well-being of friends, family and one's team. When a Filipino meets a fellow Filipino in another country, there is a bonding and

---

29 Pseudonym

willingness to go out of their way to help the other person. That resonates in teams and in organizations.

Having lived in the Philippines for five years, I can attest to this sense of care, service and warmth. However, while Filipinos may have a 'smile in their voice', one sees other emotions as well. For example, it is not uncommon to see people shedding a tear or two at the workplace. As Jon E. Kaplan, President, TDS Solutions, who was based in the Philippines/Asia for sixteen years, observes, 'People in the Philippines, more than any other country I've been in, are highly emotional. I've had three occasions where women have come to my office crying!'

Given this dynamic, leaders need a combination of skill sets to manage people, their expectations and their emotions. A considerable investment of time and effort is needed to build relationships so as to influence and lead the team. According to Lynette V. Ortiz, CEO Standard Chartered Bank, Philippines, what's unique about heading an organization in the Philippines is that Filipinos attach a high value to relationships. She observes:

> I think the approach that many women leaders, including me, often adopt is a relationship angle. I notice that when my male relationship managers have difficult client conversations, they pull me in, not only because of my position but also because I have a way of pulling in the relationship card and finding a collaborative, non-contentious way of arriving at a mutually beneficial outcome.
>
> During the pandemic, I felt there was a need to purposefully come together, whereas earlier you had unintentional conversations along the way when you bumped into people. Now, everything is done deliberately, and I work closely with the management team to make sure that we come together a bit more frequently even if it's just for check-ins.

> ### Women Leaders in the Philippines: A Perspective
>
> Carol Dominguez, President and CEO, John Clements Consultants, Inc., describes successful women leaders in the Philippines as those who have high emotional intelligence (EQ), are resourceful and will not take 'no' for an answer. In Carol's view, Filipinos are 'super high touch', and everything is personal. They are good team players and have very close family ties. Good leaders should show that they genuinely care for their people and need to 'walk the talk'.

Malasakit is ingrained in the Filipino psyche and women leaders tend to display a good blend of the cognitive capability and the emotional maturity needed. This is also more relevant in the post-pandemic world with the heightened focus on employee well-being.

While on the subject, here's a slightly different take on empathy in leadership from a Singaporean business leader, Chris Ng who describes herself as a 'passionate business partner and proud mother of two'. She shares that:

> Leadership assessments have shown that empathy is not one of my strengths! I have been given feedback that I look like a woman but work like a man! I take it as a compliment. Like most Singaporeans, my focus is on getting things done and achieving results, and not so much on relationships. But once I get things done, I make it a point to recognize people and give credit where it's due.

As is the case with leaders universally, Chris has a strong results orientation. This is evident across the board in Singapore. Whether one is talking about junior or senior roles, women are focused and super-efficient in the way they work. When it comes to how things work in Singapore, there is a pragmatic and practical mindset of getting the job done.

Another Singaporean leader, Renyung Ho, Senior Vice President, Brand HQ at Banyan Tree Group, shares her style of leadership:

How Renyung leads

> I'm very result oriented so I might drive the team quite hard, which people who are not self-initiating might find too demanding. At times, I take more effort to outline the 'why' and the 'how' as well.
>
> But what defines my leadership style most is my desire to align the personal motivation of my team to company goals. I always ask people, 'What's your personal purpose? What do you want in life?' And I align that to the work that they do. Because that's just part of bringing one's whole self to work and motivating people.

While Renyung is outcomes-driven, she uses a collaborative process to enable her team to be better aligned to their goals. Her style of delving into the deeper purpose resonates widely, particularly post the pandemic.

Balancing empathy and drive

In the examples above, we've discussed how women leaders focus on managing both results and relationships. Interestingly, research suggests that as women go up the ladder, their EQ or emotional intelligence gets better honed. This is also substantiated in the State of the Heart Report 2021,[30] which outlines trends worldwide in emotional intelligence.

---

30 State of the Heart Report 2021, Trends in Emotional Intelligence, Six Seconds

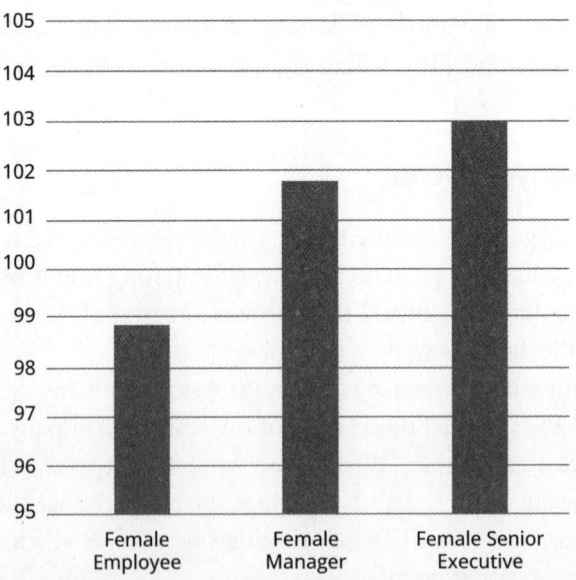

Source: State of the Heart Report 2021

The diagram above indicates a correlation between emotional intelligence and career progression for women leaders. As per the State of the Heart 2021 report, female managers score 6.1 per cent higher on total EQ than do female employees; additionally, there is a 2.6 per cent increase for senior executives. Overall, women on average are slightly better at emotional awareness, while men, on average, are slightly better at emotional management.

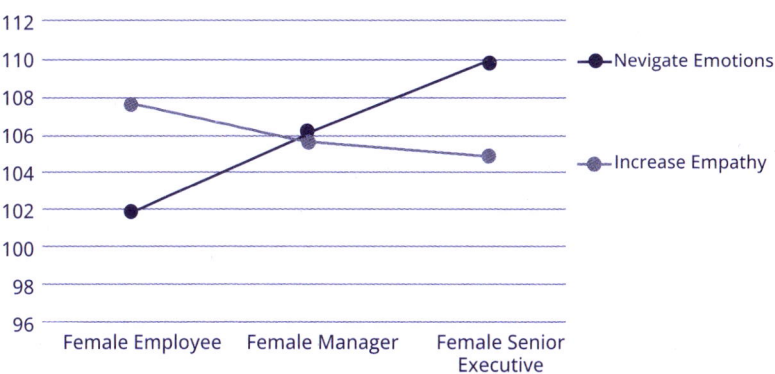

Source: State of the Heart Report 2021

The diagram above shows an interesting finding: as women advance in their careers, there is an increase in their ability to navigate or harness emotions. This correlation is not seen with men. This may also be driven by the expectations of organizational culture pushing women leaders to suppress empathy and handle increased emotional complexity.[31]

The ability to balance cognitive traits with affective traits is elaborated on by Dr Rohini Srivathsa, National Technology Officer at Microsoft India. Responsible for driving innovation and growth through 'tech-intensity' across industry and the government, Rohini shares her experience of working in the US and subsequently in India:

---

[31] State of the Heart Report 2021, Trends in Emotional Intelligence, Six Seconds

I noticed that the culture in the US, where I began my career, was different from India in some respects. For instance, being in a technical field, I found that the meritocracy in the US is held in higher sanctity. It's not that this isn't the case in India, but informal relationships also play a role in India. You may be very good at what you're doing, but you also need to have that ability to navigate the system and influence—not in a bad way, but that's the nature of the ecosystem. In India, that soft power seems to have a bigger role to play.

A hard-hitting leadership style would not take you very far in India. Having said that, as a woman you need to also be clear about what you are driving. Because there is a point until which you're going to try and take people along, but as a leader if you don't also show direction or conviction, you can be perceived as not having a mind of your own. So that balance is quite important. In another culture, you may not be penalized as much if you were more directive or less empathetic.

Indian women are extremely competent; they have learnt the value of soft power and tend to take people along. They don't get called out as much as rock stars, even though they may well be.

> The above highlights how while being cognizant of the different drivers is relevant for leaders in general, it is certainly relevant for women leaders. And taking my cue from Dr Rohini's views above, driving is an interesting metaphor to bring home the point. Does a good driver focus solely on her driving, or does she zoom out and see the larger terrain? Does she make her fellow passengers feel invested and included in the ride?

> Many Indian leaders, both men and women, display a high degree of energy and passion to make things happen. Being driven is also a necessity given the fast-paced and competitive environment. But they need to balance drive with empathy when interacting with people, which is not always an easy task. As Abanti Sankaranarayan points out, the two aspects can sometimes be in conflict. In her experience, while she tries to see things from the other person's side, this is not always easy or seamless, and she has to continuously make sure that she gets the balance right.

Emotional or rational

Gregory Rastello is an intercultural leadership coach and talent development professional who has lived and worked in France, China and Malaysia. He is of the view that women managers across these countries manage teams more easily because of the quality of the relationships they have built. He points out that, 'When the woman leader takes a decision, we follow it not as much because of the rationale of the decision but because of the quality of the relationship that we have with them.' That may not always be a positive attribute, but the point is taken.

Women leaders do bring emotion to work and make the workplace more real. That said, a female leader is often seen as being 'less rational' or 'more emotional'. For instance, Chris Ng shares how her boss perceived her to be emotional in some matters when she was being open about her feelings in order to resolve an issue at hand.

This is a common pitfall when it comes to how women leaders are perceived. In the example below, Lani Darmawan, President

Director of PT Bank CIMB Niaga, Indonesia, illustrates how she worked around this perception:

> When I joined CIMB Niaga more than five years ago, I took over a team of five thousand people under consumer banking. I was given a heads-up from HR that 'this is a man's team'—they had never had a woman leader. Eighty per cent of my direct reports were men, many in their forties. Two things that I did differently to manage the team well were: giving straightforward honest feedback and complimenting them for their achievements. Men being competitive, appreciate these gestures. My leadership style is to treat men and women the same while setting goals and expectations.
>
> While women leaders are more collaborative and understanding, so as to not to be treated as one-sided, we have to be very strict as well. For example, I track their performance and in the one-on-ones with my team, I tell them directly what I think. If they don't agree with me, we discuss further. I am a no-nonsense kind of person.
>
> We need to be able to deliver the bad messages as well. Sometimes I see men aren't courageous enough to convey a negative message. As leaders, we have to show colleagues that professional equations are different from personal ones. No matter how good your relationship with colleagues is, performance matters. Sometimes people are subservient, they compliment and send you gifts and flowers. It should not cloud your judgment. As a leader, leading by example is important; you need to walk the talk.

The above is an example of how leaders like Lani working in fairly aggressive, male-dominated bastions of banking and finance have a focused, direct and driven style of operating.

Lani's male colleague, Pri Notowidigdo, a board advisor and executive coach, found Lani to be the most successful leader in the bank in terms of her approach. According to Pri, Lani is systematic, she empowers people, she is aware of what's going on, she gives credit to those around her and focuses on benefits for all stakeholders. Her colleagues and clients like her immensely.

The postscript to this anecdote is that six months into the job, when Lani sought feedback of her performance as a leader, she was told that she was perceived as 'being very rational and even more to the point than the men'. Lani's example highlights both the strength and the pride of being a woman—something every woman should work on. Women need to be their own cheerleaders and celebrate their wins, big or small.

On a related note, Jon E. Kaplan, during his stint in Southeast Asia, found female employees to be more pragmatic than the male ones. He says, 'Sometimes males want to shoot for the top of the mountain, which is nice, but you have to take steps to get there, and I think that sometimes women can be more pragmatic and creative without getting too abstract.'

Lani's objective and focused approach resonates with Mike Liu. Mike observes that newly appointed women leaders sometimes tend to lean towards personal preference or perceptions rather than the job expectations. As a senior leader who is a mentor to several women leaders in China, Mike advises them to keep their minds free from some distractions and focus on what is required for the job itself.

Showing emotion is a positive trait that goes with the territory, and secure women leaders are not afraid to embrace their feminine side, but at the same time, they are cognizant of not overdoing it. In the final analysis, it is not about focusing on the softer aspects at the expense of results; it is about driving a good balance. Also, while women are generally perceived to be more emotional and sensitive, that may also be a factor of one's personality and less about gender.

Share, care and dare

The approach that encompasses this dual-pronged focus on results and relationships can be described as share, care and dare—possibly in that order!

Here are two leaders who illustrate this style of working.

Renuka Ramnath, Founder, MD and CEO at Multiples Alternate Asset Management, India, shares her approach:

How Renuka leads

> My leadership style is very demanding on performance and excellence at work. Doing a great job is not enough for me. It has to be distinctive and extraordinary. At the same time, I try to create a place of bonding and huge personal engagement with colleagues and their extended families.
>
> In all my roles, the common thread has been of making the workplace feel like family. I've always cared for the success of people who've worked with me. Are they growing, are they performing, are they recognized, are they happy? I have coached them, hand-held them, engaged them and shared my dilemmas with them.
>
> I build trust by putting my hand, heart and head at work and expect the same from those that work with me. I encourage colleagues to take risks, and sometimes I stand by them to clear up their mess. I expect people to recognize their mistakes and learn from them.

This is how Adele Tao, Leader, LIXIL Water Technology Greater China, describes the way she works.

How Adele leads

> I am goal-oriented and have the willingness to accept responsibilities and make difficult decisions where the future is uncertain. That means having to take the blame if things go wrong.
> I'm also competitive and don't want to lose to anyone, especially in the market. I don't take the internal targets too seriously, but I always benchmark myself and my team on sales/revenue in relation to the competition. I am determined and push myself very hard, but I also push the team. Maybe it is harsh for the team, but I tell them that it is good for them and for the company, so I am doing the right thing.
> I encourage my colleagues to celebrate the small things. Although I do criticize sometimes, I never forget to praise colleagues who make some special contributions or do good work.

There are similarities in Adele's and Renuka's ways of working and leading, in terms of how they push and celebrate performance and success—both individually and of their teams. At the same time, they stand by colleagues and take accountability when things don't work out.

New research indicates that empathy tops the list of leadership skills needed to be successful. Empathy is more effective when it leads to compassion and action, such as helping someone or making a recommendation that leads to a better solution.[32]

Illustrating many of the attributes discussed above is this account shared by Vanitha Narayanan. Based in the US, Vanitha is a senior global executive and board leader. She worked with IBM for over three decades, where she held multiple key roles.

---

32 Tracy Brower, 'Empathy Is The Most Important Leadership Skill According To Research,' *Forbes*, 19 September 2021

She summarizes her experience of working and leading markets such as Japan, Korea, China and across ASEAN:

How Vanitha leads

When you are managing multiple countries at the same time, you cannot take a 'one size fits all' approach.

When I started to work internationally, I would take the first few minutes on a call or in a meeting to establish a common context because without this clarity, people may interpret the agenda differently and can spend the entire meeting at cross purposes.

Very early on, I tried to establish with each of the leaders that I was never going to understand their country, clients and people as well as they did. However, I could help them do better in specific areas like build a better team, work with the ecosystem or with a particular client or technology. I gave them the permission and the space; I tried not to be the boss who came into town and knew it all.

Whether it was Indonesia, the Philippines or Thailand, relationships mattered, and this was a bit different compared to the US! When I did my Asia role, I probably had more client dinners and team dinners than I ever had in my life, and that was a very important part of getting to know the people and their culture and getting them to be comfortable with you.

I found that the best way to connect with the team in Korea was by bringing my expertise based on my background in telecom and making them comfortable with the language. My experience with China was that it was hierarchical in a 'you are the boss, so it's very much whatever you say' way. So, engaging with the broader teams helped to create more open dialogue and discussion. The strategies that I used were: i) establishing a relationship based on trust where I could add value to them rather than just saying 'this is how we will do it'; ii) finding that common platform; and iii) being cognizant of differences.

> The above is an acknowledgement of the diverse strategies that can be adopted to be effective in a regional role. While results and targets have to be achieved, the 'how' of achieving them is important to factor in as well. Vanitha displays a good working understanding of what this entails. In a style that encompasses both expertise and humility, she focuses on the value that she brings and the support that she can provide.
>
> Vanitha explains the context and provides the bigger picture, something that works well anywhere, but particularly when one is working across cultural contexts. Having clarity and alignment of outcomes, and an open mind to look at things from multiple perspectives, is a winning combination.

In conclusion, these leaders show a leadership style that is a combination of achieving business goals and being sensitive to the dynamics within the community. They strive to manage both the operational as well as the strategic aspects. Traits such as empathy and sensitivity, which are typically associated with women, are often perceived as clouding one's judgment or impacting rational decision-making. But the women leaders here have shown how these traits complemented their capabilities and helped them create a robust culture.

As Mike says, 'Under normal circumstances, we will be under pressures to make decisions and our intent is to make good decisions. We want to achieve the business objectives and say, "I did my job". However, we also want to be better and charming humans, and my observation indicates that women demonstrate their unique capability to connect with people at a human level.'

While the nuances of empathy are quite different from being authoritative, women have found a way to strike a balance between both aspects. At one level, saying or hearing the words 'soft skills' in the same breath or sentence as 'women' sounds trite. But when women leaders are so clear and matter-of-fact about what they bring to the table, one realizes that soft is power and real.

They said

- Women have learnt the software to not just succeed but to be effective and be good team players.
- Women leaders typically are good listeners, but they use the heart to listen to the mind.
- We solve problems together versus the 'it's your problem' approach or assigning blame. What I've learnt early on in my career is that a one-on-one conversation ending with 'How can I help you?' makes it more empowering for people.

4

Connecting the Dots

Influencing outcomes and people is a part of the job description for almost any senior leader. However, as organizations evolve, leaders are increasingly required to lead, work with and manage people who may not directly report to them. Therefore, an influencing style of leadership versus a traditional command and control one assumes greater relevance in the 'new normal' world of work.

While influencing is gender-agnostic, it requires a combination of different skill sets to be effective. That said, women may find themselves in unique contexts and situations, which they navigate using various mechanisms, some of which are highlighted in this chapter. We also discuss a few things that work effectively and others that don't work as well in the context of women leaders.

Influencing is about finding common ground to arrive at an outcome, which entails, at the outset, establishing trust and credibility. This is discussed in the next chapter. Other factors that impact one's influencing skills and abilities relate to having empathy and a good instinct about the priorities of all concerned.

In this regard, Abanti Sankaranarayanan shares a few things that have helped her influence more effectively as a leader:

> One needs to have a radar to pick up what the climate is and what is important for your boss, from a delivery and expectation viewpoint. That has helped me sense what I should prioritize. You earn the right to influence when you figure out what is important in the current organizational context.
>
> Another aspect is investing ahead in building relationships with stakeholders. Understanding them and investing time and resources makes a big difference to the building of the relationship. And this helps given the element of reciprocity in any relationship.

As can be seen from the above, there are various factors at play; one of the most crucial being identifying the stakeholders involved. This can get more complex in matrix structures spanning diverse geographies and as one goes up the ranks. At middle management, the stakeholders may be regional while at senior levels, they are often global. The higher one goes, navigating that space becomes more important. Which is when having that radar, as Abanti points out, is important.

Influencing in Asia is an art, and often, women are able to influence with or without the hierarchy.

When hierarchy is a good thing

At one level, titles perpetuate or heighten hierarchy, but they also enable women to wield power and influence. That works everywhere but particularly in Asia. A title in a hierarchical society can be a great tool in a woman's arsenal, especially in countries and organizations that are more respectful of hierarchy.

Karen Tay Koh, independent non-executive director on the boards of several companies, recounts her initial days in the healthcare space when her colleagues were senior male doctors, older than her. Karen says, 'I remember making it a point to call them by their first names to establish the thinking that, "even though you're a senior doctor, and I respect you for that, I should address you by your first name, because of the executive position I hold".'

It was important for Karen to recognize and remind herself that in the office, she had the position, the title and therefore the right to assert her position in the management hierarchy.

Leveraging the hierarchical structure can be an effective way to move things along, as Amy,[33] (name changed) a senior Asian leader, realized. Unsure of how to implement an ESG (environmental, social and governance) strategy in her organization, Amy realized that she could use the existing governance structure to do this effectively, instead of initiating a new mechanism.

With the support of the CEO, Amy created a committee that would be responsible for implementing an ESG strategy. She brought in key members of the leadership team on the committee. They decided on focus areas and got permission to form a cross-functional team that would make recommendations. She organized a few events with speakers who shared their recommendations and things cascaded from there.

In five years, they have made huge progress on this front and won multiple awards. Her learning is that rather than creating something from scratch, leveraging the existing decision-making

---

33 Pseudonym

apparatus of an organization is a powerful way to formalize and get things to move forward.

Purpose and values

Values drive behaviours, set the tone and create trust. As a male leader observed, 'When you look at women leaders, they don't talk about systems or rules first—they talk about what's important to them, such as leading with their values.'

Let's take the case of Dr Rohini Srivathsa, whose innate sense of purpose is a big factor in her being able to lead and influence a large group of people. Rohini says:

> I've realized that my own strength is in being able to lead without necessarily being a manager. I don't have huge teams that report to me, but I am able to influence a large group of people. And that has come through the ability to influence people with ideas, bringing my own energy and commitment to the table and inspiring people to learn and grow.

Another example of influencing through values is shared by Polly Ng, chairman and CEO of Global Women Connect, a non-profit social venture. Since her executive team comprises volunteers, who are free to leave if they feel that the work isn't aligned with the organization's stated values, motivating them is challenging. It is about sharing the impact of their work and getting them to see the bigger purpose.

One needs different ways to influence and lead the younger generation, who are driven differently. Polly shares how she influences the younger generation. She says, 'You can remind them to be more responsible, but you have to let them make mistakes and learn from them. Whether they are employees or volunteers, we encourage them to try different things, take some risks, give them space, allow their creativity to flow, and that's the way to influence them.'

On a related note, strategic business HR and career coach Lilian Wu shares how she leverages local values while working in global organizations. As the only girl amongst six grandchildren in a traditional Chinese family, Lilian was raised by her grandmother in Shanghai, where she began her career. She shares:

> I don't believe in doing HR for the sake of HR. My first step is to understand business priorities, people and the organization's needs. A principle I follow is 'shan wu' 善悟, which is to understand challenges with a positive mindset. I do this by thinking from the heart and asking five times 'why'.
>
> I take time to master the big picture at the global level. To illustrate, even though I have limited functional knowledge about healthcare or mechanical engineering, Shan Wu, which refers to enlightenment, helps me understand what business leaders in these industries are looking for.
>
> I aim to continuously improve and redesign HR solutions by embracing 'jie yuan' 结缘, which is a term for bonding or connection. I believe in bringing the value to collaboration or 'li ta' 利他, which is a win-win altruistic mindset that aims to create value for others.
>
> I'm willing to support others, wherever possible. I believe that if I do my best, others will follow and walk the talk. I am passionate about leadership coaching, and I believe in being and enabling others to be happy, engaged, learning and performing (HELP).

As an experienced human resources management practitioner in the pharmaceutical and automotive industries, Lilian leverages core Chinese values to create value for herself and others in a Western MNC in China.

As one has seen and learnt to appreciate in the aftermath of the pandemic, it is ultimately about the why or the *wu*!

Leveraging laterally

For four years, Dr Susan P. Chen worked in human resources in Indonesia, with its biggest ride-hailing unicorn. Of Taiwanese origin, Susan studied and worked in Europe before moving back to Asia. Her pan-European education and global experience notwithstanding, she found it a bit challenging to influence outcomes in Indonesia. In her words:

> When I started working in Indonesia, I recall having some culture shock as to how to work and influence. I was seen differently because I was aggressive and thinking of influencing change in a linear or unidimensional way in the area of enterprise transformation. That approach didn't work, so I learnt to work differently.
>
> In the UK and Norway, the leader is accountable and gets credit when she makes things happen. Working and leading in these countries is quite individualistic compared to Asia where you have to influence as a collective.
>
> As a woman in Indonesia in a less senior position, there is a lot more pressure with regard to how you can influence within the organization. I observed that it was different for the men who would often directly approach the CEO to get something approved. Whereas women leaders would influence across their peers to share the message with the CEO and then drive change.
>
> One thing that I have learnt to do differently is taking a step back. Instead of influencing vertically upwards, I learnt how to influence my peers laterally and collectively to get them to become your advocates for change. I think that is one of the biggest differences of operating in Asia.

TRADITIONAL VS LATERAL LEADERSHIP

Traditional   Lateral

Susan shares how the ways of working in a different culture impacted the way she adapted in order to be effective. Her example highlights the complexities of navigating the terrain in Indonesia not just as a woman but also as a foreigner. Having worked and lived in Asia, one realizes that there is a hierarchy of identity. Depending on one's ethnicity, age and gender, the way people perceive and interact with a person can be different, which impacts one's experiences.

The anecdote above underlines the need to quickly identify the influencers to effectively influence outcomes. This is something that Kumi Ito does well too. Kumi, a board member of several listed companies in Japan, explains, 'Every organization has a "key person" who has a great network and who is connected to other key leaders. I am very good at finding these key persons quickly. I communicate with them

> regularly, I get advice from them, and I share my ideas in the early phases. They help spread the idea and execute it. I don't care about the idea's origination or taking credit for the idea; execution is important and helps to build trust and confidence.'
>
> Amongst her many strengths, Kumi has cultivated a wide network, both inside and outside the company, which she knows how to leverage to make her case. In today's world, this is good old-school strategy that we can all learn from!

Purvi Sheth, Managing Director, Shilputsi Consultants, India, is another leader who knows the power of leveraging her network. As she says:

> I am a big believer in the 'connecting the dots' principle. In my line of work, exercising networks is critical, be it connecting people for business, to customers, for mentoring or for employer–employee relationships. This has not only helped the people who come into my world but has allowed me to broaden my horizons, add to my network and keep a legacy business running. As an entrepreneur, you have to keep finding ways to be resourceful.

Connecting the dots is relevant across cultures as well, as highlighted in Susan's example above. These cultural differences impact how women and men take decisions and influence effectively. Erin Meyer points out in an article in *Harvard Business Review*,[34] that approaches to authority and decision-making differ

---

34 Erin Meyer, 'Being the Boss in Brussels, Boston and Beijing', *Harvard Business Review*, July–August 2017

across cultures. In countries such as China, India, Indonesia, Russia and Turkey, hierarchy and deference to authority are deeply woven into the national psyche.

Also, she points out that on a worldwide scale, hierarchies and decision-making methods are not always correlated. The US is an egalitarian culture where decisions are made top-down. In top-down decision-making cultures such as India, Italy and Mexico, decisions are made quickly, but they are subject to change based on new inputs.

In countries such as Germany, Japan and the Netherlands, decision-making is a consensual process, involving a lot of people and time. Speaking of Japan, the consensual process involves *ringi*, which entails passing a proposal around level-by-level, starting at the bottom and working upwards, and *nemawashi*, which is discussed below.

Tweaking 'nemawashi'

An age-old Japanese process for buy-in and alignment that is common in organizations is that of *nemawashi,* which literally translates as 'going around the roots'. *Nemawashi* is the informal process to lay the foundations for a proposed change or project by explaining the idea to relevant people concerned, gathering their support and considering their feedback.

Jin Montesano, executive officer and chief people officer of LIXIL, Japan, shares her perspective on how she tweaked *nemawashi* to be more effective within her organization:

> For more consensus-oriented organizations, nemawashi is a critical step to smooth the way for formal decision-making. Sometimes, it can yield a totally different result because in

order to build consensus, the team believed it had to make some compromises. For instance, one could start with the idea of creating a hat, and at the end of the process, the team has got consensus to build a bowling ball.

A Western interpretation of nemawashi could be stakeholder engagement, an area that I have considerable experience in. So, while the concept of nemawashi is very familiar, my approach is to invest more in the steps that help secure buy-in for the original project or idea. I coach members of my team not to reject nemawashi but to modify their approach to make a strong business case, which includes greater awareness-building and advocacy around the merits of the desired project so that the outcome is more in line with the team's expectations.

I found some of the newer members of my team were unfamiliar with how to make the case for 'what's the benefit' to the company. I encourage them to map and identify their stakeholders: who will be for this idea, who might be against it, and how might we persuade the fence-sitters?

The anecdote above highlights the importance of stakeholder mapping and engagement, a critical skill set for leaders working in large organizations. Particularly, as Jin points out, for women who work in environments where gender bias exists but is invisible, this skill set is relevant to securing the buy-in they need to advance their projects and initiatives. By tweaking the *nemawashi* process to include an element of advocating for one's project, Jin tries to enable an outcome that is more likely to be in line with the team's initial expectations.

Connecting the dots: what works

> ### *Checklist*
> ✦ Hone a radar
>
> ✦ Identify stakeholders
>
> ✦ Connect and collaborate
>
> ✦ Manage egos
>
> ✦ Leverage purpose and values

Managing egos

'Leadership by showing respect' is often displayed by women leaders, especially in countries such as Thailand, Indonesia and the Philippines. As if to corroborate this observation, Pri Notowidigdo, board advisor, executive coach, and C-Suite executive search consultant, in conversation with me shared a few examples of women leaders who despite being a bit traditional and subservient, were able to successfully influence their colleagues.

He says, 'A senior female leader whom I respect greatly, was the CEO of a leading multinational organization in Indonesia. She would speak to me in high Javanese, which is the politest form, when she didn't have to! But that was her way of influencing me through language by showing respect to a person younger than her, often calling me Mas Pri or older brother.'

Women recognize that showing respect to peers and bosses can be simple and effective. When the above-mentioned CEO was asked what her secret was to managing male egos, she said, 'You have to play up to their ego a little bit, but not too much because they are smart as well!'

With regard to how women work around egos, here's another example shared by Xu Ge Fei:

> A woman, let's call her Madame Yu, is a successful female entrepreneur in China. A powerful, confident woman who wears high heels and make-up but when communicating with a male client, she becomes deferential. Instead of saying 'This is not working, you have to change!' she will say 'We really value your collaboration. I am honoured to be your friend and talk to you at the same table.'
>
> She will do the whole 'social dancing'. A Chinese man will seldom talk like this, but a woman is cautious because if she hurts the ego of the man, she will not obtain what she wants. That's how you play the game, and if you want to be result-oriented, you do the social dance.

In hierarchical societies, people who have the position and power, both men and women, tend to operate in a high-handed way. Managing egos and working around them requires a combination of skills.

Women may also be better attuned to recognizing brewing dissent or underlying tension. Many women leaders instinctively rely on persuasion to influence and change behaviours.

As the above anecdotes illustrate, public affirmation, tact, respect and charm can go a long way in managing a big ego. On a lighter note, as highlighted above, it may be less about social distancing and more about 'social dancing'!

> ### Pitfall: Being Present or Perfect?
>
> 'You have to be present fully and go with the flow,' a lesson that Arisa, a Thai leader, learnt the hard way. As a consultant when engaging with clients, she would always try and display her competence. But over time, she realized that it's not so much about her expertise or making an excellent presentation but about being in sync with the client and understanding what is really required so that she can deliver. Interestingly, her male business partner would remind her that 'we don't need the perfect slides, let's make sure that we are listening to the client and their agenda'.
>
> One has seen women managers and leaders trying hard to 'be the expert'. For instance, if they are in consulting, they must know the answer, even if the client is unsure of the question!
>
> When it comes to influencing, it's less about being perfect and more about being present. It's about being in the moment and actively listening. At times, one sees senior leaders fidgeting, looking away or at their phones. They send vibes that say, 'I have more important things to get to.' These are basic cues that don't earn trust.

Making it work

Renyung Ho, who is a young generation leader of a family business, shares a few things that have worked for her and a few that haven't. For instance, one thing that has not worked for her is communicating directly about issues in a group. She elaborates:

I realized that asking directly what's wrong and what's not can put people on the spot; it takes a lot for them to share. I now have smaller meetings, mainly one-on-ones, engaging them on different topics, which has helped people open up. When people see that I don't play games, I'm not political, I have the best interest of the business at heart and I also care about them, that helps to influence outcomes.

I'm starting to appreciate how being a bridge between the present and the future requires me to moderate what I say and think. So, I reframe my words and thoughts in a way that is in line with my values for the greater good. And I consciously work on taking people along on that agenda.

> Renyung has adapted her communication style so as to build trust, which helps influence outcomes.
>
> On a related note, communicating ideas simply without using jargon and complex sentences works well. The most effective communication is that which is easy to understand and relate to.
>
> And while on the topic of influencing others, being cognizant of how others are motivated or influenced can be helpful. As one may have seen or experienced, the factors that influence the influencer may not necessarily work with those he or she is influencing.

Ultimately, leading with values and authenticity is what moves the needle. This observation from Pavitra Singh, CHRO of PepsiCo India, sums it up well:

I've never felt it's different because I'm a female. As a leader, one needs to be self-aware in terms of knowing your strengths. You have to play to your strengths and use the style that works for you. For example, I've often been told that I have a non-threatening way of dealing with things. I put the person at ease and then deal with the situation. I acknowledge the other person's point of view and then share my view. I don't talk about only facts and data, I pay attention to the underlying feelings too, that's my natural way of handling situations. Whatever your style is, the intent and authenticity need to come through.

To flex or not to flex

This is a candid account of how Bonita Lee, a senior regional leader, adapts her way of leading, managing and influencing across the different markets that she works in:

> As a female leader from Asia, I had to be conscious of how I am perceived especially in cultures outside Asia and to work with them and make adjustments when needed.
>
> With Western 'MNC cultures', my experience of driving change has been through asking questions, going deep where needed, challenging and testing ideas and getting mindsets aligned before going ahead ... In terms of how performance is assessed, what you are capable of and the belief in your potential matters more than your past experience or job title.
>
> In high-context cultures, I had to invest a lot more time asking questions to understand issues and nuances more deeply. Getting to the gist of what is needed above the 'noise' but also being prepared to adjust where needed—recognizing the environment is fluid—is key to getting things done.
>
> Asia is easier for me because of my relative familiarity with the region. Overall, there is a higher acceptance of experience and competence irrespective of seniority, age or gender

although there are still some higher context countries where titles matter and have to be used selectively.

My early lessons in leadership started when I led teams across Southeast Asia; I learnt quickly that the highly pragmatic 'Singaporean style' does not work as well in places where harmony and relationships are more important. In these cultures, irrespective of the position you hold, you've first got to be accepted. Active listening to understand and then, adjusting to engage more and build deeper relationships are critical to success. I learnt early—and through some hard lessons—that leadership is so much more about winning hearts and minds of others than how smart you are or achieving your own objectives.

Later, when I lived and worked in China, I adopted a different style. Leadership agility—to be able to adjust your style to suit different environments—has been central to my development as a leader.

Overall, I've had to learn to sit back, listen and reflect before doing anything. The further you are from the frontline action, the more you have to rely on others in your team. One can't do it all alone; you have to bring people along and this varies across cultures. So, my template is not about having one style but adjusting in different places to be effective.

As can be seen from the above, one way of working may not work equally well in different environments. Bonita has learnt to flex and use a different style to get things moving in different places.

The process of influencing requires that organizational priorities as well as the stakeholders are identified. After this, one has to connect the dots and make the case, using some of the skills and strategies discussed above.

It is possible that women, before entering the workplace, may have dealt with complex or difficult situations (in male-dominated environments). In the process, they may have acquired and honed useful skills such as persuading others around them to define and balance priorities, to view things differently, and to focus on the big things. These skills hold them in good stead when navigating the corporate terrain and influencing stakeholders.

In general, and as illustrated in these examples, women leaders know how to be more encompassing and inclusive, focus on the betterment of all stakeholders, feel secure in their skin, not take credit as much but share it, placate egos subtly, know which battles to fight and which to walk away from, understand how to influence with tact, but also how to lead with a clear, relentless focus on the deliverables.

We've discussed here the ways in which leaders work in the ecosystem, using both the logic and the magic. They understand the power of tapping into a network. In some contexts, a more assertive way of influencing works and in others, a gentler style may work. Whatever gets you to the end in the most natural and effective way!

They said

- I'm very introverted but I've learnt to allow for other views before I process, to suspend judgment and avoid 'I know it all'. Talking to a lot of people helps me understand the context better.

5

Trust and Credibility

Abanti Sankaranarayanan, who worked for many years with Diageo India, shares an anecdote from her time with the company. A few years ago, a trade magazine representative asked her, 'Madam, do you drink (alcohol)?' As a senior woman leader in the liquor industry, this is a stereotype she often had to deal with. Shrugging this off, she remarked that, 'He must be thinking that it's bad enough that I work in the industry. I don't think he would have asked the same question of a man.'

Given that leadership is gender-agnostic, the way one builds trust and credibility would be similar across genders. But because women often tend to be scrutinized differently, they may need to be more mindful of how others see them and of the messages communicated through their actions and words.

The incident above, although in a lighter spirit—pun intended—indicates that when it comes to establishing their credibility, women are often seen through a different lens.

This chapter takes a look at the prejudices common to many workplaces and cultures with regard to how competence in a woman is perceived. We also discuss some aspects that build or derail trust and credibility.

As a baseline, credibility is gained through one's work being consistently good and delivering agreed-upon outcomes. Someone who epitomizes this is Indra Nooyi, former chairperson and CEO of PepsiCo. A leader who worked closely with her when he was heading PepsiCo South Asia, Shiv Shivakumar shares his view of her leadership style.

How Indra Nooyi Built Trust: A Perspective

'Indra was in PepsiCo for more than twenty years; when you spend that length of time, there is an in-built trust and credibility from rank and file, because people see long-serving people as inherently "one of them". Indra assiduously built trust with all stakeholders, from customers to captains of industry to country heads. Her unique position gave her access, and she built on that with her personal charm.

Indra would work very hard and always came very well prepared for meetings. She never took a pass whether it was family commitments or travel. In the four years that I worked at PepsiCo, she was always very well prepared for at least 80 per cent of the meetings, which is saying a lot. The gap between her preparation and that of others in her senior leadership team was a mile, so that is a standout feature.

Indra had a good ability to ask the right questions and dissect a problem. She could also judge if people were giving her the party line or knew their stuff. She was generous and would send all her male subordinates a tie every year. I still have mine.'

Shiv Shivakumar's account above of Indra Nooyi's way of working is a great example of what it takes to build trust and credibility. Nooyi's sense of purpose, commitment and pursuit of excellence were instrumental in her earning respect and success. It is amazing to hear how despite being in the top rungs of leadership, she continued to work hard and prepare for meetings

This goes to the point often made, that women have to work much harder to be noticed and recognized. That seems to be the case universally although it may be a bit different for leaders in senior positions compared to those in middle management. As Senela Jayasuriya, founder of Women Empowered Global and 1 Million Women in Power, points out, 'Women who hit the 5 per cent mark are different and are respected differently. That's not to say that they are out of trouble—there is scrutiny, but it's at a different level. There is respect because they've gone through the mill!'

Degree or pedigree

When it comes to establishing credibility, what happens when one doesn't have the credentials? In the absence of the coveted degree or pedigree of education, how can you still make it work?

Pavitra Singh didn't have a human resources degree from a premier institute in India, and her first job wasn't at one of the well-regarded multinational companies. Yet she is CHRO of PepsiCo India today, and her journey is an inspiration for anyone who believes that one always needs the required degree or pedigree of education to build credibility and a super career.

As a woman, it may not have been tougher, but it certainly wasn't easier. How did she fit in and shine? This is what she says:

You have to bring that differentiated value in your role. The most important traits are to believe in yourself and not to put yourself down. Be consistent, deliver on your promises, be very good at your work and use your strengths. Because if you are good at your job, no one will ask you 'Which college do you come from?' or 'What degree do you have?'

And now when people ask me if I'm from one of the top-tier colleges, I take pride and say, 'Actually, I'm not from them!'

The value one brings to his or her role does not emanate only from a good degree or college. That said, one has to have the content and substance—there's no substitute for that.

Across the board, credibility is earned by bringing that differentiated value in one's role, by being outstanding at one's work and by delivering on promises.

Consistency is a much-valued trait that helps build trust in a leader, as evident amongst some leaders I spoke with:

- Chris says that 'I build trust by being consistently open and direct—I don't change just because I have a bad day.'
- Rohini leads with integrity, which is about being fair, consistent, and transparent. As a leader especially in the large teams she has led at IBM and at Fidelity, it is 'the ability to consistently show people that 'she's saying what she does and she does what she says, she's fair when she has to make some trade-offs, and she shares why she is making those decisions.'
- According to Bonita, 'People have got to trust you, and that comes through reliability and seeing people through. It comes through communication and giving some of

yourself so that people know who you are and can relate to you.'

Speaking of consistency, let me share an example of two leaders of a dynamic and long-standing non-profit organization I volunteered with when I was based in Singapore.

One of the senior leaders, let's call her Claire, says the right things. She is inclusive, collaborative and wants to meet the team often and discuss ideas. But she doesn't share the complete picture, and her actions are different from her words. She is moody and inconsistent.

The other leader, whom we can call Marie, is cold, high-handed and hierarchical. She is distant and not inclusive but consistently so. I noticed that people prefer to engage with Marie since she is predictable; what you see is what you get.

Of course, as examples go, these two are far from ideal. But the bigger point is that consistency helps to build trust in a leader.

Another builder of credibility and trust is delivering on promises, elaborated on below.

Promises and pitfalls

Speaking of building trust, there are some things that are non-negotiable. Vanitha Narayanan elaborates:

> I never promised an outcome that I could not deliver. So, if it was a crisis or something we delivered to a client that was not working, I would do my best to solve it. If I didn't know what the outcome would be, I would make sure that my commitment was absolute—they would give me an A for effort.
>
> I don't make promises that I can't keep. If initially the crisis was so big or complex that one couldn't see through it,

I would make small commitments that could be met. It might be as simple as 'I am going to get you a plan by tomorrow morning. If by tomorrow I can't get you a plan, I will get you a plan for a plan.' And I would make sure that we met those commitments.

This anecdote highlights the importance of making realistic promises and following up on them. While it seems like common sense, this is a trait that is not that common and can be a deal-breaker in some contexts and cultures.

WHAT'S IN HER BAG: WAYS TO BUILD TRUST AND CREDIBILITY

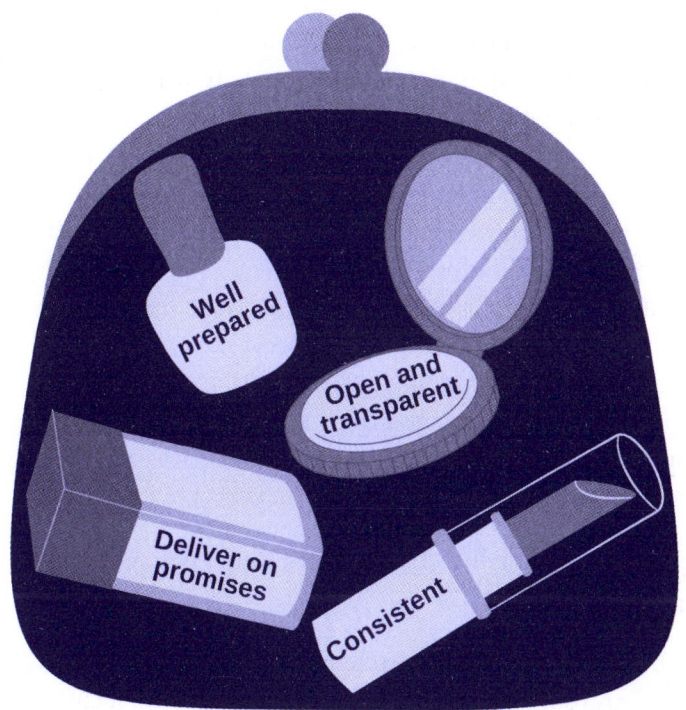

Transparency earns trust

This is an example of how Oranuch Lerdsuwankij, or Mimee as she likes to be called, managed her team in the initial days of the pandemic. Mimee is the CEO and cofounder of Techsauce Media, Thailand, and shares:

> Within some weeks of the onset of the pandemic, we realized that we had to downsize. I had to balance the cash flow, manage the employees and keep their morale up. It was hard to engage the staff without face-to-face interactions.
>
> I set up meetings with middle management and provided clear, sincere communication, sharing what the real situation was even if we didn't have the answer. We gave them weekly updates. I would talk to my mentor for advice. I couldn't sleep during that time but couldn't show my panic to my staff. Being calm helped put others at ease.
>
> We worked with our staff to develop business plans to support the best-case scenarios and worst-case scenarios. This is a very important part of managing a team and being a business owner during crises.
>
> I begin a difficult message by giving them the key message and then supporting them in terms of next steps. It's not a cut and dried conversation like "Okay, you have lost your job, here is the compensation". You have to be empathetic and treat people with respect. Transparency is the key and sensitivity is everything.

Speaking of leading in a crisis, here's another perspective. Vanitha shares:

> I don't let a crisis completely flow through to my teams, I tend to absorb and brace as much as I can whether it emanates from a client or in the organization. You give the team the comfort that you will take ownership of the situation so that

they can be open and creative and know they are not going to wind up being the casualty for it.

Something that my teams found surprising when I was in Asia was that I let them sit in on some of my tough meetings with senior leaders. I wanted them to see what I go through in real time so they would learn how I handled things positively or how I could have done something better. Also, if they saw me struggle, they felt compelled to provide me with better information the next time.

> A crisis tests leaders, and how they manage it not only shows what they are made of but also goes a long way in boosting trust in them.
>
> As evident from the above, transparency was Mimee's mantra to manage her team. In the initial days of the pandemic, when there was no manual to navigate the uncertainty, she kept the channel of communication open even when she didn't have the answers. Vanitha displays an open and approachable way of working; she doesn't sit on ceremony as the boss. She assumes responsibility and has the team's back.
>
> Good leaders lead with kindness and compassion. In moments of crisis, they step up and articulate what needs to be said. They know that taking tough decisions goes with the territory, but they are mindful of retaining people's dignity in the process. If dynamic leadership is doing the right thing at the right time and keeping everybody in the loop, Vanitha and Mimee embody it.

Trust is built around the table

Bonding over meals helps to get people to open up and forge a closer connect. Whether it's over chai or soju or laksa, connecting over food and drink is a great way of building trust across Asia.

We discussed earlier the importance of *guanxi*, which is based on reciprocity of favours and exchanging resources. When working in China, one has to invest time to get to know people and create relationships outside of work.

Greg Rastello, an experienced executive of French origin, was based in China for twenty-one years. He shares how he built *guanxi* during his time in China:

> One needs to talk a lot on the personal dimension and thereafter, go to the business aspects. You have to work on creating a trustful ambience, spending time with the team over meals, karaoke and team-building events. I would go for dinners, drink tea and spend a lot of time to get to know Chinese leaders. I did like the Chinese people—I learnt Mandarin, ate their food, learnt history, listened to songs and cracked their jokes—only then are you included in the clan, and you can make a difference.

On a related note, Sofia Shakil, an international development professional based in Southeast Asia, shares only half in jest:

> Anyone who wants to work in China should have this policy of 'don't ask, don't tell what the food is, just eat it'. You are not going to sit there and say 'Ew, what is that?' So over time, I stopped asking, 'What did I just eat?' And my counterparts appreciated this. The moment they see that you are joining them for that drink or that challenge to eat whatever they are putting in front of you, it completely changes how they relate to you and trust you.

Another example of how trust is built, or not, around the table is shared below by Nayantara Bali.

In international assignments, one can prepare and work on all the big things, but it's often the little things that can trip you up.

Nayantara's first international assignment was in Thailand where she was the hair care marketing director, ASEAN, for a leading multinational organization. Fresh off the boat from India, with a young kid in tow, her big learning was that one needs to know the value of symbolic gestures. She narrates:

> When I was working in Thailand, it was customary for my Thai colleagues to head out daily for a meal—going out for lunch was a big deal! Although it would take over an hour, I used to go along as it was a good way to connect and bond with colleagues in a more informal setting.
>
> One day, three young assistant brand managers, all Thai, approached me with their concerns. They were upset that their boss Connie,[35] who was an expat from the US, never joined them for lunch. She would eat a sandwich at her desk while all of them were out. Teary-eyed, they said, 'We cannot go for lunch freely when our boss is sitting in the office.' They wanted me to speak with Connie, who was a friend, and communicate how they were feeling.
>
> I was taken aback by the situation, but I spoke with Connie and explained the situation to her. Understandably, she was upset at their reaction since she was skipping lunches in order to finish work and get home on time for her young child. But she didn't want to offend anyone, and when she learnt how people felt about the situation, she began joining the team for lunch a few days a week. And it made a huge difference!
>
> From my experiences in both Thailand and Japan, this is a cultural aspect. In both these countries, the hierarchy is quite strong, and people feel comfortable saying what they want to in an informal setting. Which explains the importance of lunches in Thailand and the after-work drinking culture in Japan.

---

35 Name changed to protect privacy

When working across cultures, it is important to look for broad areas of commonality, but at the same time, one needs to be sensitive to individual cultural aspects. The incident narrated by Nayantara drives home how symbolic gestures like joining your colleagues for lunch can make a big difference to being accepted. Moreover, they display sensitivity and respect for cultural nuances. The little things are often the bigger things that one can trip up on, as highlighted in the above anecdote.

The Thai way of doing things is to find the right balance between head and heart; trust at the workplace is an integral aspect in many places in Asia. People have to invest time and effort in forging connections whether it's over food, conversation or common interests.

Anecdotes like the above also underline how in a different cultural context, people aren't clued in and can easily misread things. Ironically, Connie was skipping these lunches because of her family situation, which was prompting her to go home early. Yet another example of the pulls and pressures women encounter!

In another example of how trust is built around a table, we discuss how inclusive leaders encourage people to speak up. An HR leader of a company in Singapore, let's call her Marissa, shares how she would get people to articulate their views during meetings:

> As an HR leader, I have often played the role of a facilitator, helping to bring out diverse voices and opinions. For instance, when people are a bit reticent and don't say what they are thinking, having a one-on-one chat and asking a question like

'Hey Leo, you've been silent, what are you really thinking about?' helps. Over time, with trust, people will actually share.

In Singapore, it's a melting pot of different cultures and nationalities working together, and the regional teams that I worked in were a nice mix of Westerners and Asians. The Asians tend to be quieter and a bit shy about speaking up sometimes because of language and other factors.

As a female leader, you take into account the human element, you try to get people to talk through things, while perhaps an all-male team may have brushed off or bulldozed over some things.

This is an example of inclusive behaviour often displayed by female leaders, which assumes greater relevance when one works in different cultural settings.

She's got the look

As a woman, one may start off on a different footing sometimes. A senior Asian leader narrated an incident where many years ago, she had gone to Taiwan for a business meeting with her male Dutch colleague. Once there, people kept asking her if she was the Dutch guy's secretary. Evidently, he was tall, white and looked 'like a boss'. To her credit, she didn't let these perceptions relating to her subordinate bother her. But it's reflective of the assumptions people make when they think of leaders and their gender.

Speaking of looks, does age matter? When I asked Roshni Nadar Malhotra, arguably one of the youngest chairpersons in India, whether age matters when it comes to establishing credibility, she said:

It's different in the technology field because there are so many young rock stars. So, from that lens, age is not really an issue. Even if it is, the fact is that I'm here—the 'ifs' and the 'buts' don't really matter any more.

I don't have siblings. My biggest champion has been my father, who pushed me into the position of the CEO of the group company and brought me on to the board. I would ask him if we could wait some years till I learnt more. And he would laugh and say, 'It's not about your age, it's about mine!'

When it comes to age and credibility, Roshni's modesty and candour is striking. However, this may be different for women starting out and making their way up the ranks in organizations; their age is often a factor in their perceived credibility.

We discussed earlier how Susan Chen worked at influencing outcomes in Indonesia. Susan says that throughout her career, her being a female has been less of a factor; it has always been more about whether her age and looks represented her seniority and experience.

Susan's petite frame didn't exactly help boost the perception of seniority in terms of age or experience. In order to build credibility, she made sure that her voice was heard and her presence was felt in meetings, especially since she was perceived as a passive Asian until she opened her mouth. She was extra prepared for meetings so she could be fully engaged in discussions.

There is a bias in terms of the notion of looking young, something that is commonly accepted and expected in Asia. It's a strange corollary: when women are young, they should seem experienced; when they are experienced, they should look young!

Related to this is the notion of colourism—a preference for fair skin. Fair is lovely in many parts of Asia, including India and the Philippines where skin-lightening creams are popular. In a way, this is more insidious a trend than cut and dried gender differences.

When it comes to making an impression on people one meets, clothes make a statement. That's true for men but arguably more so for women. Also, women's clothes are often a subject of discussion and ridicule. Bold and powerful women like Hillary Clinton and Theresa May have been scrutinized for their choice of clothes and style. And as to the lewd remarks, innuendoes and harassment at workplaces that women universally face, that's a whole other discussion.

Olivia,[36] a lawyer in Japan, shares an experience she had while in Japan where she had a three-year-old son and a demanding job that required long hours. She would ride a bicycle to work and looked pretty flustered all the time. She was reporting to a Caucasian boss who one day remarked 'you look pretty haggard and not very feminine'. A stark contrast to the other Japanese women, who were very presentable and feminine, Olivia says that this comment stuck in her mind. She wished she had made a befitting reply, but she was younger and didn't want to be confrontational. Over the years, Olivia has come into her own and dresses the way she wants to. She is now more than capable of giving a smart retort for 'the betterment of women everywhere!'

While biases in terms of clothes aren't as prevalent in Singapore (to the extent they are in some places), a senior Singaporean leader talks of her predicament when she would travel in the Asia region. Chris Ng shares that:

---

36 Name changed to protect privacy

> In my commercial role where I am expected to meet and negotiate with customers in the region, I am often judged by my appearance even before I have a chance to sell anything to them. Some customers look out for your wedding band on your ring finger, they will also look at the dress you wear to the meeting. When I finally meet them face to face or through video calls, I make sure my attire is formal: business dress with sleeves, knee length, I ensure no deep-cut necklines and I put on minimal make-up. I also put on my wedding band, which I usually don't wear because of my exercise regime.

While Chris says this in a matter-of-fact way, it is reflective of the effort and time that goes into curating one's external appearance for a business meeting. This can be a challenge, as Punita Kumar-Sinha will agree. As senior investor and independent director on boards of companies in India and North America, she shares a concern that she grapples with:

> When I would come to India on work, one of the big questions was, and still is—how should I dress? In most countries in Asia, other than Indonesia and Malaysia perhaps, people dress in uniform (no pun intended) Western wear. In India, many women senior leaders in traditional industries wear sarees. Twenty years ago when I would wear Western clothes to government offices or public sector undertakings [PSUs] in Delhi, I would get a lot of stares! I realized that it is common for people, including male colleagues, to remark on your clothes, for example, 'You are wearing a very colourful suit, is there a wedding or a family event?'
>
> So, when I transitioned back to India in 2012 and joined board positions, this was a question I grappled with again. Would Western wear be acceptable attire as a board member, or would I be judged?

> As a woman from South Asia, I can relate to these concerns. Dress is an additional layer of complexity that working women sometimes experience in India. Many senior Indian women tend to wear saris, which gives them both grace and gravitas, although this is less prevalent in the start-up world and amongst the younger generation. On occasions when senior women wear less conservative clothes to board meetings, their clothes often become a topic of discussion!
>
> The flip side is that growing up in these environments, women are mindful of how they come across in professional settings. They have a well-honed internal antenna that holds them in good stead in uncomfortable situations.

Dress for success

But it's not always about needing to; it's also about wanting to be well-dressed! Sofia Shakil puts this in perspective:

> I am cognizant of how I present myself and come across professionally. I keep in mind who I will be meeting on a given day and dress accordingly. For example, for a meeting with government people, I would wear something less showy or extravagant and try to blend in more to connect. Whereas in a more sophisticated meeting with donors or board members, I would be dressed differently.
>
> Sometimes before an event I would get my hair done, and my hairdresser would give me either a professional or glamorous look depending on the event I was attending. As a well-respected professional, I think it's important to be well prepared in terms of the content and substance. That's a given, but I feel that as a woman, it's so important to dress for success.

> This is such an empowering stance to take! Women are often belittled for paying more attention to their clothes but as long as that's not the only focus, and it isn't over the top, why shouldn't they be bold, bright and beautiful?
>
> While women may be conscious of blending in, at a certain point, when they have the confidence and credentials, they aren't afraid to flaunt a more flamboyant style. In such situations, they aren't as impacted by comments relating to their appearance. If they are going to be judged, so be it!

The language of work

Coming back to the anecdote of Abanti that I shared earlier in the chapter, I asked her how she deals with probing questions or prejudices evident from a person's behaviour. This is what Abanti said:

> I don't know if this is an overly simplistic answer, but the honest answer is that you don't navigate it, you just shut up anyone by being very good at what you do. For example, if I'm asked the question, "What are the trends you're seeing in the alcobev industry?" how I answer in that instance, as the spokesperson or the leader of the company, tells them that I am a high-quality professional who's dealing with the subject at hand. The rest is irrelevant.

I recently read Shereen Bhan's interview in the best-selling book *The Art of Management* by Shiv Shivakumar.[37] An accomplished media anchor, Shereen states in the book that when she took on

---

[37] Shiv Shivakumar, *The Art of Management*, Penguin Random House India 2022

a leadership role, she felt that being a woman had its constraints. There was a camaraderie the men shared and an access they enjoyed that did not naturally extend to her, which made it harder to break into decision-making roles.

> Women encounter perceptions such as the above and are often held to different standards of performance. The most effective way to manage and deal with these perceptions is through one's work. In situations and contexts like the above, credibility is built through the quality, consistency and timeliness of the work one does.

This is also highlighted in an article titled 'Lessons from India's Covid-19 Tsunami' in the *Straits Times*.[38] In this piece, Ravi Velloor writes about German Chancellor Angela Merkel's departure from office: Often called *mutti*, or mother, her sixteen years in office have been marked by stability and she is credited with weathering multiple storms. In some ways, her charisma comes from her ordinariness, seriousness of purpose and predictable behaviour. Flair, looks, gifted oratory and a penchant for the dramatic are not negative traits in leaders but they pale before commitment and competence in office.

To conclude this section on a lighter note, here's a tip or trick that Chris has up her sleeve. In her role where she covers Southeast Asia, India and Japan, she initially connects with new partners and distributors over emails. She doesn't 'see' them over video calls. As she says:

---

38 Ravi Velloor, 'Lessons from India's Covid-19 Tsunami,' *The Straits Times*, 29 April 2021, https://www.straitstimes.com/opinion/lessons-from-indias-covid-tsunami

Since my name Chris is androgynous, when people receive emails from someone called Chris, they assume it's a guy. Once the initial connect is built, I suggest having a video call. And on the call, I see their reaction—how surprised they are to note that Chris Ng is a girl!

For me, this works well; over the email exchanges, I have already shown them that I can talk business. It's a good way to establish credibility. Recently, I adopted the same approach with my newly appointed distributor in Nepal. We had email exchanges and after some business talk, I arranged for a call. When he reacted in surprise, I jokingly said, 'Yeah, now you will always remember me'.

What's in a box?

Zola (not her real name) was on her first work trip to Japan to meet her colleagues. When she reached the office, they seemed surprised to see her. With her Afro hair, petite figure and definitive demeanour Zola didn't look like the leaders the Japanese team were accustomed to in the region. Not having a frame of reference, they were unsure of how to relate to her: African lady? Senior leader? Zola realized that she would need to define it for them.

First, she sought to talk to her colleagues one on one. Initially, they were reluctant to meet with her as they were two levels below their boss, who reported to her! In the one-on-ones, she told them about herself, she spoke of personal things. Family and even her hair was an ice-breaker—they had questions on how different it was, how difficult it was to manage, and whether she had (hair) extensions?

> I have heard of many topics in small talk and polite conversation, but talking of hair in a work meeting in Tokyo sounds surreal! However, the conversation made Zola's colleagues feel at ease and got them to open up and ask questions, which was a great start given the cultural inhibitions. Later in the evening, when Zola noticed the women were working late, she told them to go home; she empathized with them as she had an eight-year-old child too. They couldn't fathom her—who was this African woman leader who was both empathetic and dynamic, who spoke from her head and heart?
>
> Whether we admit it or not, we all have some unconscious biases, preconceived notions or associations based on things we've heard, seen, experienced or read about. The anecdote made me wonder if it is easier to conform to the 'boxed' perception that people have of us. Or is it easier sometimes to attempt to shape the box?
>
> Zola's story is a good example of the latter as she went about being herself in the Land of the Rising Sun.

Finally, being authentic

Women sometimes struggle with striking the right balance between their external 'professional' appearance and their authentic, natural self. Being authentic is being aware of *who you are* and *why you are doing* the things that you are doing. This is what some leaders shared about being authentic:

- 'I feel that celebrating wins and owning up to losses and failures make for authentic leadership.' – Lynette Ortiz

- 'I am being natural. When I talk to colleagues I often enquire about their family. And the next time I meet them, I refer to the conversation and ask them about it. It is real and that comes through.' – Anna Cortes

In conclusion, let me share what Carol Dominguez said when I asked her, 'How can women be authentic yet effective?' Her reply was succinct and super: 'I think that you can be more effective if you are authentic.'

One can see, smell and sense authenticity with all 'good' leaders—male or female, local or expatriate. It is a game-changer anywhere, as well as in Asia. Here's to women who are not afraid to be as they are—smart, confident and colourful icons of leadership.

Making it work

To summarize, these are some things that women leaders do to navigate perceptions around trust and credibility:

- They earn their stripes by being good at what they do. They focus on developing their capability and competence, above all else.
- They take accountability seriously and deliver on promises.
- They balance competence, warmth and strength. They make the effort and take the time to connect with people, forge relationships and make them feel included.
- They develop a thick skin as sometimes the best response is to let one's actions speak.

- They are present, actively listening and engaged in the conversation or discussion.
- They are transparent and honest especially during challenging times.
- They are themselves.

They said

- 'If you want to lift the performance of the organization, you have to lift yourself...my message to my team was always meet my bar, and that bar would constantly be moved up.' – Indra Nooyi[39]
- In certain places, the expectation of women is different. I recognize that I don't have the visual needed, so I try to speak without video. I use my voice more effectively.

---

39 From an event organized by the Growth Faculty to talk about Indra Nooyi's autobiography, *My Life in Full: Work, Family, and Our Future* https://www.thegrowthfaculty.com/blog/Indranooyiquotes

6

Fitting In and Standing Out

Sunsanee Supatravanij narrates a humorous anecdote relating to her experience as an Asian woman leader in the UK some years ago:

> I was in one of Unilever's product meetings with the top global managers in London. We were discussing strategies to boost sales of haircare products. As I looked around, seated at the table were older white men, with little or no hair, talking about innovation for Asian women's hair. It struck me that as the only Asian woman in the room, I was the only person who had some real understanding of the hair issues that we were discussing!
>
> The senior management at Unilever was a big boy's club twenty to thirty years ago. Initially, I worked on getting accepted, but after a while, I realized that I would never actually fit in the boys' club. My learning over time was that it was less about fitting in with them and more about feeling comfortable and confident in your own skin.

Managing downwards in Asian cultures is not much of a problem. It's the sideways and upwards that you need to work on, and that's probably the challenge for women. In terms of managing upwards, you will never be one of the boys. But what I learnt from my experience is that your bosses feel comfortable with you when they see you as a valuable member of that team. As a woman, you need to figure out how you can be perceived as a valuable team player and contribute as one.

> As Unilever's global brand director, strategy and innovation, Sunsanee was one of the first Thai female leaders to represent Unilever in the UK. Since the organization was 'more Western', being both Asian and a woman was a double whammy as she 'stuck out a bit more'.
>
> Her anecdote highlights the importance of celebrating the different perspective and value that a woman brings to the table, a table that seats a majority of men. Sunsanee underlines how it's important for a women leader to think in terms of how she can be perceived as a valuable asset to the team. Strategizing how she can contribute will not only enable her to be successful but also enable her to earn her team's respect and trust.

Many of us can relate to being the only woman in a course, room or department. It's not all bad, but it's certainly something you remember. I recall once being a part of a senior leaders' meeting—an old boys club if you will, a group of older men who had known each other for ten to fifteen years and spoke the same language. It was cliquish, and one couldn't really be a part of it especially being new, young and female.

In this chapter, we discuss how women navigate these situations. We explore some real-life experiences, discuss a few strategies that women use and share their learnings.

Being in a man's world

Punita Kumar-Sinha, an experienced investment manager and corporate governance expert, talks of how she managed being a woman in a man's world:

> When I joined the world of finance, I was one of a handful of Indian or non-white persons in the investment industry. For a while, I was a novelty. It was a different culture and wasn't easy to fit into. Years later, when I became partner, I was one of five women partners in the entire firm and one of the only Indian women partners in a Wall Street firm.
>
> Because I was a minority woman, I had to excel in what I did, and I had to go the extra mile. I started off as a quantitative fund manager as there weren't many quantitative fund managers at that time, and I could excel in that with my PhD and engineering background. Also, I was an early investor in emerging markets and ran one of the first few India funds globally, which helped me make a niche for myself.
>
> I am a straightforward, direct person and generally have no problem giving tough feedback or asking tough questions when needed. My tough style is also partly due to the fact that I ended up studying with a male cohort, in a male-oriented profession and organization. When you are the only woman, you aren't taken seriously unless you start behaving like the men. So subconsciously I imbibed a lot of the characteristics of the people around me.

Here is another account of managing in a 'predominantly' male environment in the US. Lynette Ortiz shares her learnings and experience:

When I began my career, I was the only woman on the trading desk in New York. I learnt not to be thin-skinned in the uber male-dominated trading room. I didn't want to be the angry female always taking exception to comments that were not politically correct! For instance, my colleagues would joke 'Don't have your dogs around Lynette' because they thought that all Filipinos eat dogs. Granted there are some provinces where this is prevalent, but certainly most Filipinos don't eat dog meat! Anyone would have flown off the handle, but I didn't take these comments personally.

Having gotten used to all the banter in the trading room made me tough and helped me build a constitution to deal with men and their language. On coming home, I learnt to call out certain things but not in a shrill manner. The ability to keep calm in the face of challenges as a female leader helped me a lot.

> Given that women are often perceived as being emotional, the ability to be calm and carry on are qualities that hold Lynette in good stead as she rubs shoulders with alpha-male honchos in the world of banking.
>
> Another observation is that since the older generation of women was in a minority in the workplace, they felt that they had to behave more like men in order to fit in. This was Punita's case and the case with the older generation of Japanese leaders, as elaborated upon in the chapter 'Don't Talk Like a B@#$%'. Punita focused on her work and strove to build competence in a niche area. She was strategic and at times deliberate about her career choices.
>
> Sometimes the best way to stand out is to fit in.

> In a recent training session I facilitated, a Middle Eastern leader shared how she was often not included in post-work meet-ups over beer with her international teams when they visited the Dubai office. This, despite being the boss!
>
> Not losing sleep over incidents like these, women figure their way around. It takes tact, tenacity and as Lynette says, a bit of 'thick skin'. As the only woman or one of a handful of women in a meeting, one observes the rules of engagement, understands the tone at the top and adapts to the cultural code in a way that feels authentic.

My observation of these women leaders is that many of them downplay their gender. They don't fuss, whine, expect special treatment, or want to be singled out. Rohini Srivathsa sums this up well:

> I recall my husband once telling me: 'You might forget that you are a woman but others in the room are probably seeing you as one!' Despite being a woman in a male-dominated industry, I tend to be focused on my work and the impact I create, and I'm not as conscious of my gender. Whether it is technology, strategy, or the ability to build relationships, I'm bringing all of me to the table, not just the woman to the table.

Using the outsider card

In Asia, there is a hierarchy of identity and a hierarchy of differences, which can make it challenging for the outsider or foreigner to fit in. In some places, there is even a term for the foreigner—in Singapore, white persons are referred to as *ang moh*, in India they are called *gora* and in Japan, foreigners are the *gaijin*.

Jin Montesano, who has lived and worked in Brussels, Singapore, Bangkok and now Tokyo, puts this in perspective when she says:

> When you are non-Japanese, you are basically put in the 'foreigner' bucket. As a gaijin, the principal difference is that I am a foreigner, and other attributes that make me different seem quite secondary. So, to some extent, my gender, race and age seem to matter less because I am first and foremost a gaijin. Some people see it as a disadvantage, but I have always thought of my 'outsider' status as a kind of 'superpower' because it gives me unique permission to challenge norms, bring my own perspectives to the table, and support change.

One advantage as a foreigner, regardless of gender, is that one gets a licence to say things that others may not be able to or want to. For Olivia, an articulate lawyer of Japanese origin, being perceived as a *gaijin* allowed her to be a bit more vocal and aggressive when she moved back to Japan after some years in the United States.

Speaking of adjustment issues for people repatriating to their own country, having experienced this first-hand, I can attest to the fact that it isn't an easy transition. Punita Kumar-Sinha, who transitioned back to India after thirty years in the US, feels like the outsider in both places. In her words, 'she fits in to both India and the US to a point and doesn't fit in to either, after a point.'

Build your brand

A proactive and powerful way to fit in and stand out is to work on developing a personal brand in terms of what one stands for and what differentiates one's leadership style or way of working. Building a brand for an entrepreneur is probably easier as she has her own rules to make and follow. But in an organization structure, there is a culture and a structure, so in that context, developing one's personal brand requires some effort.

Abanti Sankaranarayan elaborates on this: 'The point of standing for and reflecting a few skills that you demonstrate consistently and well, becomes your signature as a leader and evolves into a bit of a brand. And that's what people should focus their attention on when building a brand. For instance, something I have consistently done is display the ability to find solutions to very complex problems whilst working with people.'

I recently heard that Abanti wears a saree to work daily. In her earlier role as the chief strategy and corporate affairs officer of Diageo India, Abanti felt that her choice of attire reflected her eye for detail, love for aesthetics and affinity for tradition. Above all, a senior leader dressing in Indian attire in a British MNC in the alcohol beverages industry certainly makes a statement about what she stands for.

To blend or not?

On a related note, I asked Jin Montesano about whether, given her larger than life persona, she feels the need to blend in in the Japanese MNC she works for in Tokyo. This is what she says in her characteristic candid style:

> If you spoke to my friends and family, they will probably tell you 'Jin is not someone who can blend in very well.' This isn't because I'm a woman, necessarily, but simply because of who I am. For example, I talk very fast and loudly, yield a kind of frenetic energy, and am almost too boisterous for many environments. Of course, I am mindful about not disrupting or creating chaos, and I have been given feedback about dialling it down or adjusting myself throughout my career. I

have managed to make some progress, but I prefer to try to be my 'most effective true myself' as much as possible.

If I do not feel accepted or included in an environment, I will work to gain acceptance as I am. If it is not possible, I tell myself that there will be other paths that allow me to work and live a more authentic life. I have in the past changed companies because the culture was not right for me. I try to be who I am as much as possible, toning some aspects down or up depending on whether it is necessary to be effective. For example, in a more formal culture, I may speak more softly than I normally would.

A key takeaway from Jin's comment is the need to be deliberate but authentic and true to oneself. This is not easy as one tries to fit in in an organization, especially if the culture is not conducive. And as women, it isn't always easy, as highlighted by Melinda Gates in her book *The Moment of Lift*.[40] Melinda talks of her initial years at Microsoft where she found the culture brash, argumentative and competitive. She was toying with the idea of leaving Microsoft when this question came to her like an epiphany:

> Could I stay at the company and be myself? Still be tough and strong but also say what I think and be open about who I am—admitting my mistakes and weaknesses instead of pretending to be fearless and flawless and above all finding others who wanted to work the way I did?
>
> What I realized much later, paradoxically, is that by trying to fit in, I was strengthening the culture that made me feel like I didn't fit in...In workplaces around the world, women are made to feel that they aren't good enough or smart enough.

---

40 Melinda Gates, *The Moment of Lift: How Empowering Women Changes the World*, Flatiron Books, 2021

> ... It can take women a long time to realize that the bad fit we're feeling is not our fault but a fact of the culture.

Melinda goes on to illustrate how she turned things around for herself at Microsoft and summarizes it as:

> ... being myself and finding my voice with the help of peers, mentors and role models ... It's expressing your talents, values and opinions in your style, defending your rights and never sacrificing your self-respect. That is power.

This leads us to the topic of organization cultures and some ways in which they impact leadership styles, expectations and preferences.

Organization cultures

I was privileged to speak with Yousuke Yagi, a highly respected male leader in Japan, regarding women leadership in Japan.

> As the CEO of People First Ltd, Yagi points out that smart women with high potential don't want to join Japanese companies because of their discriminative practices with regard to age, seniority and gender.
>
> In traditional Japanese behemoths, promotions are driven more by seniority than performance. In this context, Yagi sheds light on the 'membership system', so named by a researcher, Dr Keiichiro Hamaguchi. This system, which entails lifelong employment and is seniority-driven, is one of the biggest roadblocks to promoting diversity in Japanese companies. Yagi points out that when female workers take maternity leave, it impacts their chances of promotion under the seniority-driven system. As a result, many talented females, especially those who can speak English, avoid working in Japanese companies and join foreign companies.

As seen above, Yagi shares how unconscious biases and the seniority system are obstacles to women's careers in Japan. The preference to work in multinational companies does not hold true only for Japan. Many of the women leaders I spoke with across Asian countries, expressed their preference for working in multinational companies.

An interesting example of making a transition from a global MNC to a local organization with a country culture is that of Sunsanee Supatravanij. For eighteen years, she worked for Unilever, which was based on a matrix of regional, global and local structures with interwoven hierarchies. For her, one of the highlights of working in this culture was learning to find similarities and synergies to build on. Subsequently, when Sunsanee joined a Thai organization as a director, she began to experience Thai social norms (see Chapter 7) in a way that she hadn't earlier whilst working in an MNC. She felt that both these experiences were enriching and brought her perspective full circle.

Lilian Wu, who has been working with a French MNC in China since 2011, feels that the combination of Chinese agility and French innovation helps to move things forward faster and better. She appreciates the commonalities between French and Chinese cultures—such as both cultures having a long-term approach, which works particularly well in the field of human resources.

When we speak of inclusion, it is about bringing one's whole self to work and being able to put forth one's ideas without the fear of being misjudged or misunderstood. When women are encouraged to speak up and share, it helps move the needle on feeling heard and being included.

From all accounts, women managers and leaders felt that MNCs provide more freedom in terms of expressing career development goals and bringing different opinions to the table. One leader talks about how, as the only female leader in the commercial business unit of an American organization, she felt lucky to be given the opportunity to take risks at times and try something new.

Working in an American MNC has given another leader the opportunity to ask questions and sit at the table with senior stakeholders, whereas in a less progressive organization culture, she may have been expected, or even asked, to stay quiet and follow instructions. Of course, this cannot be said of all multinationals; it depends to a great extent on the culture and the leadership team. But by and large, women leaders felt that in organizations where the local/country nuances are more pronounced, there are differences in day-to-day aspects such as who sits at the table, who gets invited for some of the strategic conversations and how decisions are taken and communicated. Such factors impact their growth as compared to working in a multinational organization.

Martha,[41] who heads a large business in Southeast Asia, says, 'A culture that encourages creativity and independence has helped shape my career; given me the freedom to think out of the box and grow. I learnt over time that I work well in this sort of environment—not in overly authoritarian environments that value a lot of hierarchy and order.'

---

41 Pseudonym

Fostering a culture of inclusion

Roshni Nadar Malhotra, shares a few of her challenges and experiences related to creating a more inclusive organization after becoming chairperson of HCL Tech in 2020:

> HCL, unlike most Indian tech companies, which were founded in south India, is one of the only tech companies founded in north India. Our business has people from different walks of life and cultures. So, we have this huge intercultural play with leaders and employees from both north and south India with different leadership styles.
>
> I have a south Indian [Tamil] father and a Punjabi mother, I live in Delhi, and I grapple with the cultural nuances every time I go to Chennai in south India. Culturally, you realize that when you work in a country like India, apart from cricket, there's very little that's commonly threading you together!
>
> In the past few years, we've encouraged and embraced diversity at all levels including on the board. We had only one-woman director since HCL was formed, and now there are four women directors, including me, which is a pretty good number for Indian companies. That brings a certain diversity on the board, and in discussions and views, which I really like.
>
> Also, we mandated each of our twenty-five top leaders or corporate officers to have at least two direct women direct reports. This has not been easy to accomplish. You have to start changing the engine, one layer at a time, to make sure more women rise. Some of this is done organically and some is mandated from the top.
>
> Another way to create a culture of inclusion is to consciously have more people attend meetings and give them the opportunity to speak.

As is apparent from Roshni's experience, there is huge complexity and diversity involved in running an organization in India. Creating long-lasting change and impact takes time and effort, and as Roshni highlights above, some of this is done organically and some is mandated by senior management.

Allies across genders

An entrepreneur shares how in her experience of running a business successfully over the years, men have been supportive and encouraging, actively championing her endeavours. This is as it should be. Men, as husbands or fathers, play an important role in the success of women in this part of the world. For many women, their first champions are their grandfathers and fathers. In her autobiography *My Life in Full*,[42] Indra Nooyi credits her *thatha* or grandfather for igniting her lifelong interest in reading and learning.

Given that men are the majority group in workplaces, they need to be cognizant of the biases that exclude or discourage women and address these behaviours appropriately. As pointed out in an article[43] by Elisabeth Kelan, managers need to reframe the recognition of inequality as a learning opportunity, not an exercise in assigning blame. When managers start noticing gender inequalities, they should point them out to others and facilitate corrective action.

This is what some male leaders had to say in terms of how they support women colleagues:

---

42 Indra Nooyi, My Life in Full Work, Family and our Future, *Hachette India*, 2021

43 Elisabeth Kelan, Why Aren't We Making More Progress Towards Gender Equity?' Harvard Business Review, December 21, 2020

- 'What I've learnt is not to cut women off, without meaning to, when they're in a free-flowing discussion. You need to listen a lot more.'
- 'As a "champion for diversity" in the organization, if I spot any biases in the room, I immediately step in and address them in a public forum.'
- 'I make sure to drive a concerted and active focus on developing women managers for roles we have identified.'
- 'I involve women in every decision-making process and have their voices heard.'
- 'I ensure that my HR department finds ways to harness the talented qualities female leaders bring to the group.'
- 'We made female talents feel that "we have a future together here".'

Leading from the front, these male leaders don't shy away from making their workplaces more inclusive for women. Empowering one gender should not be seen as a dilution or loss of power for the other gender, but as a win for both.

Speaking of allies and empowerment, do women have each other's backs? Undoubtedly, many women, as they go up the ladder, mentor, advise and promote younger women managers. They share their learnings, mistakes and advice. But there are instances where, for a variety of reasons, women don't support one another. Which is a shame given the journey that women are on. Perhaps they can lean on each other more, going forward.

As Purvi Sheth of Shilputsi, an HR consulting firm says, 'Women leaders of today should really think about opening doors and giving more opportunities to women. Not because they are women—they still have to prove themselves, but they can certainly open the door to opportunities and growth. Because we are in those positions now to do that.'

Finally, who can say it better than Madeleine Albright, former US Secretary of State, when she remarked, 'There is a special place in hell for women who don't help other women.'

In general, women tend to be more conscious of feeling included, or not, probably because of their journey and since they are fewer in number.

When people feel excluded, they react in one of two ways: either they keep quiet and accept it or they stand up and make their presence felt. Here we have seen examples where women reached outside their comfort zone but not to the point where it didn't feel genuine or authentic.

These women recognize that it is less about fitting in and more about feeling comfortable and confident in their own skin. As Sunsanee says, 'The learning I had was that as a woman, you need to work on "you" to make it an enriching experience for you and everybody you interact with.'

Ultimately, to stand out, you have to know what you stand for.

How they stand out

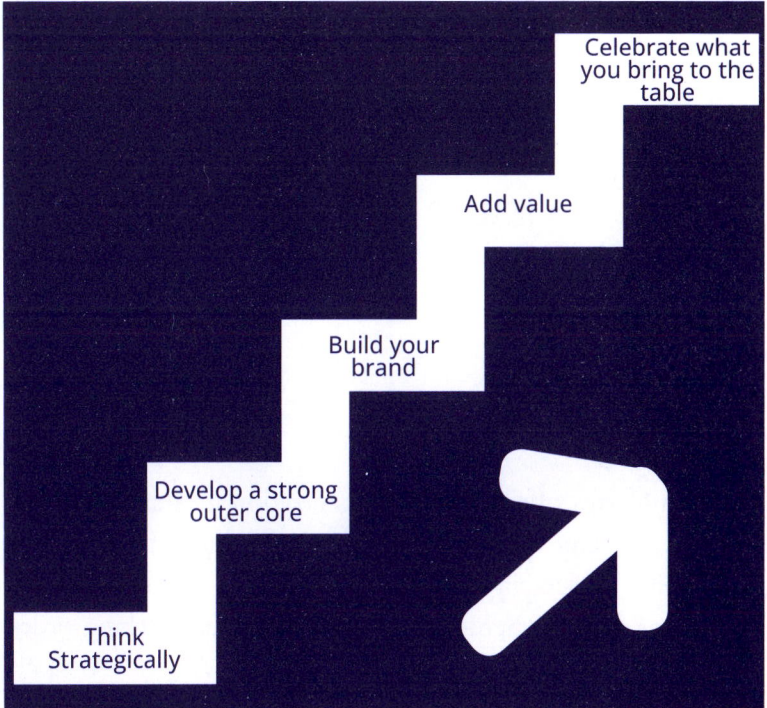

They said

- I don't think one should act entitled, but if a stereotype or bias is giving you an advantage that is not unfair, seize it and move on.
- As a woman, it's about knowing what's your truth and being comfortable in that. You define who you are.

7

Visible and Vocal

Anna Cortes[44] heads a large organization in the Philippines. She narrates her experience of attending global meetings where, like leaders in similar roles, she had to reconcile her country role with where she fitted in the global pecking order. In her words:

> In the country role, you are the boss, and everyone looks up to you whereas in the global setting, you are one of many, and you have to make sure that your voice is heard. In my younger years, I recall going to a conference in Europe and feeling intimidated and thinking, 'If I say something stupid, they will remember "that Asian woman" because I am the only one!' But I taught myself that if I could be remembered negatively, I could also be remembered positively as 'that woman from the Philippines'. Over the years, I harnessed that positivity and tried to boost my self-belief. Wherever possible, I would

---

44 Pseudonym

volunteer to talk on a topic. Even though I would get very nervous, I forced myself to speak, and that's how I became more visible in a global setting.

This anecdote has a parallel with the one shared by Sunsanee in the earlier chapter. What struck me in both these examples are the similarities: both are women leaders from Southeast Asian countries working for multinational organizations, grappling with fitting in and making their mark. When I heard both experiences, I had to remind myself that twenty to twenty-five years ago, working across cultures wasn't as commonplace as it is now. In a sense, both these women were ambassadors of their countries and genders.

Anna etched a place for herself by speaking up and becoming more visible in an international setting. Needless to say, this is relevant in any setting.

In this chapter, we discuss some pitfalls relating to how women speak, yet don't always speak up. The chapter also contains insights around finding one's voice that women leaders have learnt in the course of their careers.

The articulate woman

Vanitha, who worked in a regional role in Asia, makes an interesting observation. She felt that many of the women she interacted with across Japan, Korea and China were more comfortable with speaking in English than their male peers. She attributes this to their natural ability to adapt, which led them to work harder on their communication so as to be more successful at work.

Speaking of English skills, one has come across a large number of women, (and men) in Asia who are proficient, particularly from places such as Singapore, the Philippines and India. However, while women may be articulate, they don't always say what's on their mind. In meetings, they are seen as 'talking too much' or 'not talking enough'. They often tend to qualify their viewpoints with apologetic caveats or subtle disclaimers. As a senior woman leader said, 'Do women have the ability to share an idea that is theirs and clearly own it without diluting it in any way?'

Whether it's contextual or cultural, on one level, women can have no problem expressing themselves; on the other hand, they often hesitate to speak up. The many faces and facets of women!

Being Asian

At the risk of stereotyping, communication is muted and nuanced in Asia, especially in contexts that are collectivist and hierarchical. Karen Tay Koh illustrates a few examples reflective of the ingrained mindset:

> The constant challenge I have is communicating in the face of opposition or in the face of differences and to be able to stand up rather than just run away. For instance, I felt that a recent transaction conflicted with a board position I hold. I was worried about it and this kind of built up in my head. Later, I spoke with the chairman of the board whose advice was, "Well, you really shouldn't run away from addressing the issues. Communicate openly and honestly." That was great advice because my instinct is always to run away in the face of conflict.
>
> As women, we have this fear of conflict. And being Asian, we are brought up to be obliging people who don't like to offend. My learning is that I need to deal with real or imagined fears. Because of this learning, I now work more on my communication, but issues still come up.

> The above anecdote highlights how the Asian conditioning to be respectful and non-confrontational can be a double-edged sword when it comes to expressing disagreement or dissent in a corporate environment. This is also associated with feeling 'shame' or 'loss of face', highly prevalent and manifested across Asia.
>
> Karen's experiences are real and relatable, and they highlight the need for everyone, including women, to confront their fears and concerns.

Pitfall: being modest is good

Related to the above is the tendency of female leaders to be harsher or more conservative when it comes to how they evaluate their achievements. For instance, Adele gives herself a much lower score in a self-evaluation than her bosses, peers and direct reports give her. Like many women, she tends to be more critical or conservative when assessing personal capabilities whereas in general men tend to be more overt about their achievements.

Olivia recalls her experience of appraisals in her younger years. Always on the receiving end, she says that she was almost apologetic in everything she did at the workplace. When her colleagues asked, 'How do you think you did?' she would say, 'I have a lot more to learn …' There was no way she would say, 'These are the things I have achieved, so give me a promotion or a raise!' Absolutely not! Seen through the cultural lens of being a woman and a Japanese woman at that, Olivia would underplay her achievements and look at her faults. Over the years, Olivia has learnt to be more assertive and express her aspirations better.

The tendency to be modest and understated is manifested in different forms across Asia. As Xu Ge Fei puts it, 'Chinese women look for harmony and peace, not confrontation. They consider themselves to be the earth and men are the sky. They receive the water and sunshine and fertilize life. They are passive, which is not always seen as a positive quality! You will hardly ever see a Chinese woman saying, "If I can't do this, who will"? She will likely say "I will do my very best, I will try to achieve this goal, I understand what you are saying."'

Thai women consider themselves to be equal to men but also describe themselves as 'adaptable'. As an HR director of Thai origin says, 'Being a Thai woman is more about being adaptable; you have to adapt to fit in to the role that may change over time and also the expectation that may change over time.'

Self-doubt and confidence: making it work

A person who exhibited some of the aforesaid traits was Himari[45], a senior Japanese manager. When she was promoted and included in the organization's senior leadership team, she was intimidated initially. This is her account:

> The leadership team comprised Japanese men and foreigners, and as the only Japanese woman, I was overwhelmed. I struggled initially to express myself. There were times when I cried at the thought of speaking in front of these senior leaders.
>
> Fortunately, I had an executive coach, which made a big difference. My coach made me reflect on how I would like to be perceived in meetings. Every time I had the leadership team meeting, I would tell myself, 'This time I will behave

---

45 Pseudonym

like this.' Coaching helped me adapt to the mindset of a senior leader, and gradually, I started feeling more comfortable. I began taking greater ownership of my subject area and realized that in that room, I was the most knowledgeable on certain subjects. That realization made me feel better, and when I began speaking with more confidence, I was perceived differently by the leadership team members. They found my views valuable, and they began trusting me.

> Himari wanted to fit in with the leadership team, but she also wanted to stand out as somebody who was smart and had a mind of her own. Having ownership of her field and trusting herself to speak knowledgeably was her way of carving out a place for herself. She realized that it is possible to feel both included and respected for your insights even if you are the youngest, least experienced person on the block.
>
> This anecdote is a reminder of the unspoken, unseen turmoil that often underlies external appearances. This is more prevalent with women at all levels, who, despite portraying an outwardly confident façade, grapple with these anxieties. It also shows how coaching can make a huge difference to mindsets and behaviours.
>
> This is also accentuated by inherent cultural traits of restraint and reticence. Olivia points out that Japanese women tend to have an inner face and an outer face, and don't express themselves until they feel comfortable.
>
> When it comes to 'leaning in' and taking a seat at the table, it begins with finding that confidence to express oneself. This gets easier over time; as women build their confidence and their constituency, they (learn to) hold their own.

Related to the above is the aspect of preparation for a meeting. Whether it's at junior, mid-management or senior levels, women tend to prepare much more before a meeting. As a woman leader said, 'However much you know as a woman, you always feel the pangs, "Do I know enough?" You want to go into a meeting 110 per cent prepared, and that means that you will do a lot of research, you will check for best practices elsewhere and you try to get the lay of the land.'

While this level of preparation enables them to boost their confidence by spotting gaps and improving their competence,[46] it can also be a pitfall that women should be cognizant of. Driven by the 'perfection gene', the focus on 'getting it right' tends to put a lot of pressure on women. That said, this could be less of a gender thing and more of a personality thing, but there does seem to be a tendency for women to sometimes miss the forest for the trees.

The flip side of being confident is that if one overdoes this, it can come across as being arrogant and high-handed. Leaders, especially women leaders, are often a bit circumspect and reticent in the initial days and months of a new job. But as they grow in confidence and in the role, they should be mindful of not going the other way. From all accounts, knowing one's capabilities and being mindful of the gaps can serve to keep leaders confident and grounded.

Unlock the voice

Lynette Ortiz, CEO of Standard Chartered Bank in the Philippines, observes that:

---

46 Tomas Chamorro-Premuzic and Cindy Gallop, 'Leadership Lessons Men Can Learn from Women, *Harvard Business Review*, 1 April 2020

Women often have this false sense that they are privileged to be in the room as opposed to [having the] right, resulting in the tendency to over-prepare so as to not be the 'dumb blonde'. I am more confident about asserting myself having done this for many years, but at junior levels, women feel hesitation to speak up. The pressure is worse in the banking industry since senior leaders are usually men.

> Lynette's observation of women hesitating to speak up in meetings is on point. Also, one has seen how in the cacophony and noise of a meeting, women avoid speaking and recede into the background. At times while speaking, if someone else speaks louder or cuts them off, they tend to desist from making their point. Needless to say, this also depends on the company or environment one is in.
>
> Vanitha makes a great case for speaking up. She tells the women she mentors, 'If you are uncomfortable making a point, remember it's not about you, it's about the idea, it's about the project, it's about the client, fight for that. You are not just fighting for yourself.'
>
> Women feel uncomfortable making it about themselves. But the moment they make it about something bigger than themselves like the team or the organization or a cause, they become passionate and committed. As Vanitha says, 'That is a way for women to have their voices heard. We always talk about the seat at the table, but we don't talk about the voice at the table; yet that is how decisions get made.'

Pavitra shares how she's often observed that in meetings, women will not take a seat at the table—literally! They choose a seat behind the conference table, not around it. Whether it's a cultural thing or a lack of confidence, she thinks it's symbolic because it indicates that one doesn't want to come into the conversation. An inclusive leader will call out to people to take a seat at the table, which is a small but impactful gesture.

Another leader shared how when attending important meetings, especially when the audience is not familiar, she comes in a few minutes before the meeting begins. That gives her some time for initial interactions and to build rapport with others, so that one is not 'going cold' into the meeting.

Getting people to open up and share their thoughts during meetings and discussions may also be culturally driven, as discussed below.

Peeling the mask

Sunsanee began working with a local Thai company after working with Unilever for eighteen years. She shares her experience:

> When I joined a Thai organization as a director, I began to experience Thai social norms in a way that I hadn't earlier whilst working in an MNC. I realized that there's much more respect for authority, and politeness comes with that. Another aspect that I had to learn to work around was that people are less forthcoming in their ideas and their opinions in Thai organizations. So you can be in a meeting where the only person speaking could be a boss!
>
> It's not as if people don't have ideas or thoughts, it's just the way that they choose to express and feel comfortable to express. 'Kreng jai', or this feeling of being overly considerate comes across all the time in Thai culture. People are always overthinking that they, or the other person, will lose face. They put on a mask, or a shield that you have to peel and work through.
>
> As a director on the board of a Thai company, the question that I struggled with was: How can I bring out the creativity and openness in people so that it adds value to the discussion?

Especially given that the key to success in Thailand is 'through and with people'.

I found that being a leader, one of my key roles was about creating a supportive space and enabling people to come forward. I had to be able to get them to answer, 'Would this be a good way, or would that be a good way? What do you think?'

I organized smaller groups and workshops where people could dare to say what they didn't in big groups. And to enable this, one has to work behind the scenes as well. One has to create opportunities for more synergy because synergy doesn't happen on the table; people don't debate or disagree there!

This is a great example of adapting as a leader to the hierarchy-related nuances of reticence and respect. In general, Asians tend to sport a mask (pandemic or not). Given the collective nature and inherent reticence of the Thais, Sunsanee is mindful of the need to create a safe space, so that people feel comfortable in speaking their mind and exchanging ideas.

> This experience is not exclusive to women leaders but the fact that Sunsanee is mindful of nuances like this and finds ways of working around them shows her perceptiveness and adaptability. She recognizes that in Thai society, creating the right kind of ecosystem is key.
>
> By and large, women leaders create a safe space. But is there a downside when the environment is too safe or 'trusting'? My experience is that while it's important to create an environment where people feel safe, it should also enable people to do things differently and learn from mistakes. If that is not the case, the leader should be able to step in and course correct or make small adaptations to the way of working, while retaining the core spirit.

Be calm and succinct

In the run up to the 2021 Tokyo Olympics, comments made by Yoshiro Mori received wide media attention. Mori, who was the head of the Tokyo Olympic organizing committee was quoted as saying women talk too much and that meetings with many female board directors would 'take a lot of time'. This led to a series of events and eventually, Mori had to step down from his position.

Speaking of communication in Japan, Kumi Ito, a board member of several listed companies in Japan, says she advises young students and working women to make a short but impactful comment at the right time. A message that is short and said with respect works. A long-winded, loud, shouting style or protesting 'no, no, no' doesn't work!

Kumi's advice to her female colleagues to keep it short and sharp is on point. Research indicates that women speak, on average, three times more than men in terms of words. So, while women managers and leaders may have a lot to say, they would appreciate that being succinct is an art worth honing as well.

Broadly speaking, and as seen from the above, when it comes to communication in Asia, what is important is the manner or *how* one speaks up to be effective.

As discussed earlier, this is relevant given the need for harmony in Japanese society. But in other cultures too, the way one communicates the message is important. It is not so much *what* women say as *how* they say it.[47] The emotion needs to be

---

[47] Kathryn Heath, Jill Flynn and Mary Davis Holt, 'Women, Find your Voice', HBR *Guide for Women at Work,* Harvard Business Review Press, 2019

dialled down to ensure that the style doesn't take away from the content. Speaking deliberately and evenly in a measured manner seems to be effective.

In a lighter vein, an Asian leader says: 'I speak slower. I speak lower. I use fewer words, which has greater impact. Men can only take in so much, so you have to get to the point quickly because they simply cannot take it otherwise!'

Under the radar

Related to this is the manner in which women express ambition.

In general, Asian women express a desire to 'move up the organization' in more gentle and guarded ways. As a director of an MNC in Singapore mentioned:

> The conversation is subtle versus what I've seen with men. It's good to put up your hand and sign up for more participation or projects, but in Singapore, people feel uncomfortable doing that. I've had people reacting, saying, 'Don't bring attention to yourself' or 'Are you trying to be the boss's favourite?' In society, sometimes it is seen as being in poor taste to be overly ambitious and raising your hand to do things. Which gets more pronounced in the case of women—it's an additional layer.

If subtlety is the operative word in Singapore, in Thailand it is humility. Arisa explains:

> I believe that if you do your best, you will get what you deserve. Never ask for it, but it will come eventually if it's yours. Perhaps Westerners feel comfortable to openly express their aspirations, but in Thai culture, we have been brought up to be humble and not overconfident, which influences when it comes to careers too.

> Clearly, the line between what's acceptable and what's not is a thin one in Asia.
>
> While ambition isn't perceived to be unpalatable, how it is expressed depends on the individual, organization and circumstances, and the broader societal norms do influence how it is communicated and perceived. As a senior woman leader says: 'How women speak up needs to be contextualized in the culture—because if you come across as this brazen, ambitious woman then you've blown it!'

'Why me?'

While on the topic of ambition, women may say, 'Why not me?' but they also say, 'Why me'?

Lynette narrates a recent incident where she was on a regional call to discuss the selection and nomination of managing directors.

'As leaders, we were asked to weigh in, and after a shortlist was compiled, the question of managing the male-female ratio came up. I said, "Of course that's an important point, but the number one factor in the selection process should be competence. Who deserves that seat?"'

As she points out, 'I don't want to be the "token female" CEO. I don't want to be ungrateful, but I want to be there because I deserve it.'

'Why me' is also an important factor for Kumi Ito when she is considering a decision for the next challenge or position. Since it is becoming more common to having women directors, she gets a lot of offers for the position of external director of companies. But when she is approached because she is a woman, she tells them to please find someone else. As she says, 'I would like to join the board for my strength or competency like substantial marketing experience, leading diversity programs, or finding a new cloud based approach, not on the basis of my gender!'

Although the practice of appointing women directors to enhance gender diversity is becoming more common, leaders such as Lynette and Kumi want to be chosen for their expertise, not because of their gender.

What women could do more of: take charge

'Promotions will happen because my efforts will be recognized.' This is a myth, as elaborated upon by Jin Montesano, who has years of experience working and managing teams in Asia:

> I often come across this assumption among some women that if I put my head down, work hard and get things done, someone's going to recognize my hard work, tap me on the shoulder and say, 'You are doing a damn good job, I am promoting you!'
>
> This does not happen very often in real life. Though I have not conducted any study on it, my experience has been that more women than men believe in this kind of mythical reward system.
>
> Women need to find ways to be seen and heard in the workplace; volunteer for the stretch assignments and advocate for the critical experiences that will enable them to grow and develop as professionals.

> One reason why women don't express ambition or lean in is because they feel 'I am comfortable' so they don't want to try harder. It's the good versus the great thinking—'it's good enough, so I am content to stay at this level'. Another reason is because of lack of awareness of opportunities within the company or outside. Women are often focused on their current role or job and are not necessarily wired to look

externally for opportunities. Being alert, agile and proactive is important, especially in a post-pandemic world.

Women tend to let their work do the talking and often get passed by. Being vocal is not about showing off. It's about letting people know that 'I am the leader of this team, this is what I am doing, and I am doing a great job!' On the flip side, one has also seen women leaders who flaunt their successes needlessly. These behaviours can sometimes detract from their well-deserved accomplishments.

Many of the woman leaders I spoke with for this book had one thing in common—they had great role models, mentors or bosses who saw promise in them and gave them wings to fly. Role models matter, particularly for women. They demonstrate that success is possible and inspire women to aim higher.

Chris Ng, who has always proactively reached out to mentors through her career, says, 'You can't wait to be noticed. You have to take charge and make things happen. It helps tremendously if one has sponsors and mentors who advocate for you, but at the end of the day, the person in the driver's seat needs to be purposeful. No one openly says that they want a promotion. How did I tell my boss what I wanted? By telling him what I didn't want! I told him that if I got another role, I would give it my best. It's about communicating how I can add value to a role that I've never tried.'

When it comes to networking, a common pitfall is that women feel shy or feel they don't have the time or energy to invest. Women should network smartly and strategically. Vanitha puts this in perspective: 'In the earlier years of my career, I needed to be home for my daughter, so whether it was rounds of golf, or going out for a drink, I didn't network because time was important. But what I believe is it's important to find ways to be connected into diverse networks because that helps to broaden your perspective.'

Vanitha makes a valid point when she says that 'Having information is no longer having currency because everyone has access to information, but how you are able to connect different pieces of information to develop more relevant points of view or actions is what is going to differentiate a great leader from a good one.'

In conclusion, women need to be their own cheerleaders, something that many women find hard to do, because it feels like inauthentic self-promotion. Woman managers and leaders need to find ways of speaking up in their own way. They need to be vocal in order to be visible.

In some conversations with expatriates based in Asia, they felt that help in the house and family support were huge factors that allowed working women in Asia to work and balance their lives in a way that is different from women in other places, allowing them to better focus on their career.

While that is true, I'm not sure if outsiders also saw and appreciated the other side—the inequity that Asian women may be grappling with, quietly fighting their own battles at home and work, while not wearing them on their sleeve, sarong or sari. They may have support outside the workplace, but the journey at the workplace is one that only they traverse. And if they do this with hope in their hearts and fire in their belly, more power to them!

They said

'When you're a leader everyone watches—the way you walk, talk and smile. You must do it with confidence.' – Indra Nooyi[48]

- Based on my experience and observations, I would say women leaders are patiently assertive.
- My default as a female is to listen first. Women scour and get the temperature of the room before we venture an opinion. Sometimes I catch myself and say, "Why are you waiting, say something" because by nature I am introverted.
- Role models nudge you along and give you that confidence. You see them doing things on their terms and you also see what not to do.
- Women have to raise their hands more. It will not happen by default.

---

[48] From an event organized by the Growth Faculty to talk about Indra Nooyi's autobiography *My Life in Full*, https://www.thegrowthfaculty.com/blog/Indranooyiquotes

8

The Good Women of Asia

Sofia Shakil is an international development professional currently working with The Asia Foundation where she heads the country programme for Pakistan and leads the work on economic development across Asia.

Years ago, after working with an 'American' organization, she joined a multilateral institution in Southeast Asia. She recounts her initial days and shares her experience:

> A few days into the job, I recall my manager telling me, 'You have to learn to behave more Asian.' And I was like, 'I am Asian. What are you talking about?'
>
> I realized very quickly that he was implying 'if you want to excel in this organization, you have to put your head down and nod. Even if you have something to say, don't be the first one to say it. Let some of the older people or the men go first.'

And I thought, 'Wow, this is a big, big difference from the professional organizations I've come from.'

It's not like the manager was saying that that's the right way. He was saying that that's how you get somewhere as a woman here, an organization that is 'Asian'. Over the years I would constantly hear rejoinders like 'You have to be patient; you have to wait your turn' on everything. What was interesting to me was that I wasn't looking to impress; I was just doing my job. My conversations with other female colleagues also suggested that we would get labelled as being too impatient or too ambitious if we raised our hand and said something that was said normally, not to impress anyone! And we often saw that women who got promoted to leadership positions were those that often (not always) carried those 'Asian' characteristics.

This candid account by Sofia, who has more than two decades of experience working with the World Bank and the Asian Development Bank, has some interesting takeaways.

One observation is in terms of how expected behaviours are strongly influenced by the culture of the country or organization. In this instance, while the organization was based in the Philippines, the culture of the organization was driven more by East Asian influences.

This anecdote gives rise to the question of what constitutes 'Asian' behaviours or values, especially those relating to the acceptance of and impact by a woman leader. The title of the chapter stems from the ingrained patriarchy in many Asian countries where women are expected to behave in a certain way and do the 'right thing' from a societal viewpoint. In this chapter, we discuss the broader sociocultural context of leadership and explore how women leaders navigate the norms and expectations.

The landscape: norms and nuances

Societal norms, stated or not, define and shape women's careers in various ways. For instance, they may impact the industry that women choose to work in. In some places in Asia, it isn't common to see women in commercial and front-end sales roles, which entail a fair amount of travel and meeting customers, many of whom are men.

In terms of the jobs that women can or cannot do, it varies across Asia. Let's consider Thailand; a friend shared how when he took a pre-booked taxi from the Bangkok airport, he was surprised to see a Thai lady driving it in the wee hours of the morning. Similarly, in China, it is not uncommon to see women security guards at airports routinely frisk male and female passengers, something that is unthinkable in many places in Asia.

Notwithstanding these examples, it isn't a smooth or seamless journey for women. They encounter various societal or family beliefs such as the expectation of getting married by a certain age, a huge determinant of career trajectories and success.

In many places in Asia, power distance is quite pronounced. Even though most organizations have flattened, there are strong associations between power and titles. Authority in not just the professional domain but also in the social and personal domain is more skewed towards one gender. As Punita Kumar-Sinha says, 'In certain situations, if I speak in the same manner as my husband, I will not command the same authority that he does. Just by virtue of being a man, he carries more authority in India.'

In professional and social interactions in parts of South Asia, there is a tendency to 'slot' people to figure out who you are and where you belong. When filling out a form in India for a bank account or for any government-related service, one is required to provide either one's father's name or husband's name. One is framed as per the two male figures in one's life! From a South Asian perspective, there certainly is a more prescriptive upbringing. I recall a scene in the Bollywood Hindi movie *Queen* where the lead actress Kangana Ranaut openly belches in a taxi in Paris, something she could not and would not dare to do back home, because that's not acceptable behaviour for good girls.

On a related note, sociologist Dr Emi Kataoka of Komazawa University has said, 'In Japan, women are treated only as supporting characters to men.' However, I found it interesting to learn that Japanese women are pushing back against a tradition where they were expected to buy chocolates for their male workmates as part of a tradition called *giri choco*—literally, obligation chocolates.[49]

And here's a perspective on Chinese women shared by a successful Chinese professional I spoke with: 'Chinese women are still carrying an invisible gilded cage through which society and family judges them if they don't work, if they work too much or if they don't work enough. They have to be capable but not too capable, pretty but not too pretty and they will be judged for their confidence. It's a culture cage—you see this in everyday interactions.'

---

49 Justin McCurry, 'Japanese women push back against Valentine's tradition of "obligation chocolate",' *The Guardian*, 11 February 2019

Super women

Marie-Therese Claes, Professor and Head of Institute for Gender and Diversity in Organizations at WU Vienna University of Economics and Business, lived and worked in Southeast Asia for twelve years. She observes that women in Southeast Asia may have a senior position at work but at home, they're still the wife and mother and responsible for the household. She points out that, 'This sort of tension between these roles is evident in other places too. But because of the cultural aspect and Confucianism, it is bit more pronounced in Asia.'

An Indonesian male leader feels that Indonesian women are expected to be superwomen in that they should be good professionals at work and when they come home, they should serve their family. These expectations are prevalent in many places in this part of the world. I found that the importance of 'balance' between individual and family responsibilities was a recurring theme in the narratives of women leaders across levels.

One of the fallouts of the pandemic has been the resultant disparity in the division of domestic work in households across the globe; these are particularly glaring in some societies. For instance, men in Japan do fewer hours of household chores and childcare than in any of the world's wealthiest nations.[50] As Yousuke Yagi points out, 'the mindset of many Japanese people is that "men do work, and women do housework".'

Socially and culturally in Asia, women have learnt to separate their two lives. As Marie-Therese says, 'At home they may serve their husband in a certain sense, and at work they can be the boss.

---

50 Motoko Rich, 'Stuck at Home, Men in Japan learn to help. Will it last?' *The New York Times,* 16 May 2020

For Western eyes, this would be a contradiction, but in Asia, it is not necessarily a contradiction. They manage to seamlessly combine these roles.' This ability is certainly prevalent in this part of the world. Some years ago there was a popular advertisement in India where at the end of a working day, the boss in office is cooking for her husband at home, who is her subordinate. This advertisement encapsulated the mindset where the Indian working woman, and in this case, the boss, seamlessly switches to being the good wife and mother at home. While behaviours and expectations are changing amongst the younger generations, Indian women often bear the brunt of managing home and hearth more than women in Southeast Asian cultures do.

Clearly, a change in mindsets and a more equitable approach to sharing housework would enable women to have a better balance (at the very least) between their professional and personal lives.

'Is she ready?'

When being considered for promotions, it is usual for candidates to be assessed if they are 'ready for the assignment' amongst other things. And while the readiness is also assessed for men, the scrutiny is greater for women given the cultural dynamics. For instance, in parts of Asia, depending on the organization culture, readiness is determined by asking women candidates about their matrimonial status and family members including children.

Elaborating on this is Shiv Shivakumar, Group Executive President, Aditya Birla Group. Shiv shares an anecdote highlighting the mindset during his stint as chairman and CEO of PepsiCo South Asia and how they worked to address this gap:

> When we were revisiting gender diversity and inclusion, we realized that the hiring managers would ask female candidates questions like, 'When do you plan to get married? When do

you plan to have a kid?' Interestingly, these questions were never asked of the male candidates!

We realized that we had to actually educate men in terms of how to talk to women during the interview process. We had to train them not to ask such questions. We communicated zero tolerance on these aspects and sensitized people about this. And this was effective. Over time, as a result of these interventions, we saw much better traction of women wanting to join the company.

As seen in this anecdote, deep-seated mindsets impact perceptions on women's capabilities to take on roles. These biases and perceptions regarding marriage and kids may be more pronounced in the Asian context because of the emphasis on family values and filial responsibilities. These are factors that lead to the 'leaking pipeline'. In organizations worldwide, women's numbers reverse as they go higher up the ladder because many women opt out of their professions when facing the transition from middle to senior levels of management.

On a related note, as per a glass-ceiling index compiled by the *Economist*, which ranks twenty-nine countries on ten indicators, East Asian women face a ceiling that appears to be made of 'bulletproof glass'.

As per a joint report by Google and Bain & Company on women-owned enterprises in India, the challenges women face in building a business include problems in raising capital and not being taken seriously. This has wider resonance; Mimee, founder of a start-up in Thailand, concurs that availability of funds is one of the biggest challenges women face when starting a business. She points out that while most industries are male dominated, to see a woman founder in technology companies is rare, almost like a cultural norm. She says, 'Out of about 500 start-ups, only thirty or forty in Thailand are led by female founders, and they face difficulty in raising funds due to preconceived notions of investors. So, we need more venture capitalists who understand this pain point of female founders.'

Not all biases are negative, of course. In some jobs and industries, women have the edge. In front-end, client-facing jobs, for example, there is often a preference for women. Women are seen as more approachable, easier to work with and more understanding. Of course, these preferences are driven by biases of another kind—but that's a topic for another time.

Fragile: handle with care

Across South Asia and Southeast Asia, one comes across many women managers and leaders who are dynamic. In some cases, they have had a privileged upbringing with access to opportunities and good education, often a Western one. On the surface, they seem smart, articulate and able to hold their own, but often one finds that this confidence is fragile and skin-deep.

Some months ago, I was invited to speak to a cohort of senior women leaders in Asia as part of a mentoring programme for them. In addition to my session, I attended a few others out of an interest in the subject. I noticed that some of the themes that repeatedly came up were around self-doubt, how to be assertive and how to establish credibility. Given that this was a cohort of successful and talented women embarking on a journey to take their careers to the next level, I was a bit surprised to see how much of the headspace was occupied by conversations around the need for approval and validation.

However, much has been written and spoken about how women tend to have more self-doubt than men and that women often underestimate their abilities while men overestimate theirs.

In more patriarchal societies, women are encouraged to 'adjust' and seek approval from male figures of authority. Practices such as these that begin in childhood are reinforced in adulthood, fostering feelings of self-doubt and poor self-esteem.

A related point is the 'need to please' tendency that is prevalent amongst both Asians and women. A Filipino leader I spoke with shared an incident that may resonate with readers, as it did with me:

> Years ago, when I was a new manager, I had to ask people to come in to work on a holiday, which wasn't appreciated. In order to please my team, I ordered pizza for everyone. And I heard one of the people loudly comment, 'It's bad enough that we are working on a holiday, but she doesn't want us to go out for lunch either!' This is a classic example of no matter how good your intentions are, you cannot please everyone.
>
> This simple experience taught me a lot because I no longer try to please everybody. Life can be simpler if you just ask people or do as you please!

When it comes to ambition and leaning in, women often have their own reservations, as to what they can and cannot do, over and above societal biases. As an HR leader observed 'It's true when they say that men raise their hands even if they're 50 per cent ready while women will wait because they want to make sure that they are at least 90 per cent ready'.

If we are discussing self-doubt, can 'impostor syndrome', which refers to doubting one's abilities and feeling like a fraud, be far behind? Andy Molinsky, professor and author, suggests one way to navigate this is to recognize the benefits of being a novice.[51] This is a good starting point as it enables one to bring

---

51 Andy Molinsky, 'Everyone Suffers from Impostor Syndrome – Here's How to Handle it', *Harvard Business Review*, 7 June 2016

a fresh perspective and do things in ways that others haven't thought of.

Having discussed a bit of the sociocultural landscape, let's move on to how women have worked around some of these norms and expectations. The dynamic between hierarchy, patriarchy and relationships resonates throughout Asia. So, for managers and leaders, it's really about finding that sweet spot amidst these nuances. Following are a few stories and strategies shared by the women leaders I spoke with.

Navigating the norms

Tweak and adapt

Kumi Ito has worked for Sony, IBM and GE Healthcare Japan. She was the CEO of 4U Healthcare (4UL), a start-up in the healthcare space for five years. Interestingly, when she started work after her studies, her passion was to be a jazz singer! She has been a professional singer since she was twenty years old, and she still regularly performs in Tokyo. This is her account:

> Some years ago, I joined 4UL, a venture company with a relatively flat organization structure, as CEO. My colleagues didn't care about hierarchy or gender, but the leaders of the parent company who had worked in traditional Japanese companies had a different approach. So when I came on board, they tried to lead and guide me on every aspect. It was very stressful, but I remembered my earlier experiences in IBM and GE where initially, too, there were similar challenges.
>
> I focused on getting small contributions for the boss, my team and me. I tried to improve the sales and consulting phases and showed the team better ways to engage with clients. When the team realized these worked, they started to support me. It was great to see, over time, the change of

mood in meetings. Today the situation is totally different. I lead several projects, which they support. Their behaviours are still conservative, but they consider me as a valuable and collaborative person.

I don't want the hierarchy to be used in the room or on the project. I tweak my approach; when talking with a client, I adopt a more formal and respectful tone. But when I communicate with my team, I use a more friendly style. I ask them not to call me CEO Ito Shacho, but to call me Kumi-san or Ito-san. Some men feel uncomfortable with this as they are used to the hierarchy.

And here's another take on her leadership style, shared by Shojiro, who has worked with Kumi in a previous organization. Shojiro Mitsuzawa is the CFO of Integrity Healthcare, a healthcare technology start-up in Japan.

How Kumi Leads: An Outsider's Perspective

'I think Kumi is good at communicating with men in a positive and charming way without confronting them. Many female managers are too self-conscious and try to fight against men, but she is able to involve men as her allies in a very natural way, which is a very special skill. Even men who didn't have a good impression of her at first often ended up becoming her fans because they sympathized with her logical and interesting stories full of humanity.

She is very considerate to those around her and is willing to make bold decisions at times. When she makes bold decisions, she carefully explains the background and reasons behind it, which makes it easy for others to sympathize with her. She can express her opinions very well to anyone, whether it is her boss, subordinate, or colleague.'

> As seen from Shojiro's perceptive observations of Kumi, she exhibits a combination of a bold decision-making style along with the ability to connect in an endearing and humane way. Despite being a senior leader with much experience, when Kumi was being scrutinized initially, she kept her composure and focused on getting the small wins. This helped her build credibility and gain trust.
>
> The description of the traits and skills that have facilitated her success is interesting as seen through a male lens, especially considering where Japan lies on the spectrum of women's leadership and empowerment.

Working around the dynamics

Roshni Nadar Malhotra heads the Shiv Nadar Foundation in India, which aims to create an equitable, merit-based society by empowering individuals through transformational education. Her work for the foundation has taken Roshni to remote areas in the Indian heartland, where the cultural landscape is different, and one needs to adapt to be effective. She puts this in perspective:

> When working with different stakeholders, you have to figure out the dynamics of culture and what works. I quickly change the tone and manner of speaking, as well as the language. I realized that having a command of the vernacular is so important!
>
> Another aspect in a hierarchical culture is how you seat people in the room. I might be the head of the foundation, but I don't necessarily need to sit at the head of the table. You realize that where you sit is really where you stand.
>
> This is not being submissive to individuals, but about being cognizant of culture. One has to keep one's eye on what is the end goal. My end goal is not to try and make them respect me more and feel self-important; it is to get my job done.

Roshni illustrates how she uses her understanding of the nuances, including verbal and non-verbal cues, to adroitly adapt to a situation. She is focused and doesn't let the dynamics of power and other people's priorities get in the way of her accomplishing her end goal.

Recognizing unconscious biases

Pavitra Singh took a six-month sabbatical at a time when it was an aberration in the Indian corporate world for a woman to take time off for anything other than maternity leave. She resumed work with a renewed perspective and an appreciation for the importance of speaking up at the workplace more often. Here is one of her reflections:

> Every time there was a discussion in the office about having an offsite, the task of organizing it would get delegated to me; I was used to hearing 'She will handle it'. I decided to speak up and asked my boss why I would always be expected to manage mundane tasks when there were other people around. As a senior manager, it certainly wasn't my job description!
>
> And he said, 'No, it's not that. When guests come home, typically my wife takes care of the hospitality because she's good at it.'
>
> So this bias of women being naturally good at managing certain tasks got transferred to the workplace without my boss realizing it. It led to stereotyping me and other women colleagues. Fortunately, he understood my viewpoint and in fact thanked me for this learning, which he said he would keep in mind in future interactions with women colleagues.

This incident highlights the need to call out unconscious biases. Only when one is shown the mirror can the process of awareness and change begin.

Learnings as a male leader

- 'When I would tell my colleagues that I am going to pick up my daughter, I would get this look from my managing partner and colleagues. I didn't care, because I learnt that from women—they would be frank and honest in a gentle way about their need to balance work and life.' – Pri Notowidigdo
- 'As a man, you need to recognize women's personal responsibilities, and I've been guilty of not doing this a few times. I think giving space for that is important if you're a leader leading women.' – Shiv Shivakumar

Stay calm and carry on

If in some places the discussion on gender emancipation has become loud and shrill, in Asia, the mantra seems to be 'stay calm and carry on'. In the words of an interviewee: 'The gender factor will always be there. We accept it as a fact of life and carry on. That may be the Asian mentality.'

Asian women may not rave and rant when they are held to a different standard or seen through a slightly different lens. As Marie-Therese says, 'I think women navigate patriarchy and societal expectations without making it public and without "seeing" it. They just do it; they don't fight or make a big deal about it.'

However, when needed, they do make a statement. In 2019, Yumi Ishikawa, a Japanese model and temp worker, highlighted the practice of female workers in Japan being required to wear high-heeled shoes to work. She gathered 18,000 signatures on a petition and went on to become the public face of Japan's

#KuToo movement, a pun on the Japanese words for shoes (*kutsu*) and pain (*kutsuu*).[52]

On a big picture level, it seems that in the West there are more legal and institutional structures and mechanisms to lower barriers and raise awareness whereas in the East, the onus seems to be more on the individual to navigate. That said, it depends on the organization, its culture, the leaders and the importance they give these aspects.

In a sense, women who join the workforce in parts of Asia have already negotiated the traditional boundaries and battled the demons within in ways unique to them. In this regard, Sofia Shakil shares her viewpoint:

> For the modern-day South Asian women, social status provides a privilege that gives us more room to manoeuvre. To elaborate, if you are in a professional or leadership role in Pakistan but come from a well-off background, with an elite education and having broken many social barriers, you are in a different kind of operating space than if you were a lower middle class working woman who suffers the brunt of biases.
>
> As a female professional, one learns to make use of that operating space to thrive in professional environments that may not be conducive to supporting diversity.
>
> I believe that a female leader has often had to speak louder to be heard. She has had to develop a broad and tall stature, often brought upon by what could seem to be a borderline aggressive tone, to get a fair seat at the table. This may be true globally, but it is even more amplified in Asia. So, for women who do make it to positions of professional leadership, it's not

---

[52] Motoko Rich, 'The Japanese Rebel Who's Fighting the Tyranny of High Heels', *New York Times*, 10 December 2019

surprising we have an armor of tools that we have acquired along the journey.

Gender stereotypes, cultural norms and values impact opportunities, careers and success. This is not unique to Asia, but it is certainly prevalent and women are cognisant of the underlying hierarchical and relationship dynamics in society and at the workplace. They tend to be respectful and polite; yet they can be demanding and assertive in their own way as and when needed.

WHAT'S IN HER BAG: TOOLS TO NAVIGATE

Visibility matters

The cultural bias is reinforced by the lack of role models and women in senior positions, which is why promoting visibility of women who have successfully navigated these cultural barriers is one way to reduce them. A strong advocate of this visibility, Atsi Sheth shares her viewpoint. Atsi is Managing Director, Global Head, Credit Strategy and Research, Moody's Investors Service, and is based in New York. This is her perspective:

> Like many of us, I have anecdotes where others' behaviours reflected conscious or unconscious biases around gender and sometimes ethnicity or national origin. But I was able to largely shrug these off thanks to how I was raised, by parents with a strong commitment to fairness and who were fearless about challenging bias when they saw it. Also, having seen successful Indian women since childhood, my starting assumption was that women could thrive in a wide range of professions. For example, growing up, I had a working mother, and the prime minister of India was Indira Gandhi.
>
> So, I tend to see gender bias as a problem for the one who holds the bias, rather than the one towards whom it is directed. But I recognize that shrugging off bias isn't easy, and my ability to do it reflects my privileged upbringing.
>
> In the corporate world, when people look at the lack of people like them in senior ranks, it can be disheartening. If you are at a junior or middle level and don't see leaders above you that look like you, you question if you will end up there. Lack of visibility reinforces cultural bias. Promoting visibility of women who have successfully navigated these cultural barriers is one way that the barriers themselves erode a little bit.

> So, as I get older and more senior in my role, I see it as my responsibility to be visible, to ensure the ladder I am climbing is extended and accessible to all. I attend, mentor and speak at different forums because I know it's really important to showcase that visibility.

For women leaders who grow up seeing strong women in their family with independent voices, it can be hugely inspiring. In her account above, Atsi highlights how empowering it is to see women with access to equal opportunities and the freedom to make choices. In a sense, visibility is self-perpetuating; successful leaders encourage and empower others down the line to do the same.

In this chapter, we discussed how women leaders effectively work around norms and negotiate what matters to them. Given the complex dynamics and expectations, women have to navigate a complex path. While some norms can be worked around, not all can be addressed or resolved.

Atsi puts this in perspective: 'Overhauling long-existing gender norms, in society and the workplace, will take time. Whether in Asia or in the West, successful women recognize existing norms but don't necessarily feel that they have to adhere to or perpetuate them. Success itself lies in recognizing norms, but not letting them become insurmountable career obstacles or a crushing burden.'

Changing ingrained mindsets is obviously not easy and will take time and effort. Women take this in their stride and recognize that ultimately, it is a journey.

They said

- Behind each Chinese woman, there is at least 200 years of history, legacy and culture and one can see the different generations' imprint on them.
- If you're in an environment which is not progressive, then you blend in because that's the norm and that's the way you think you should behave.
- Women in the West are in a different place on the journey of women's emancipation. In Asia, with the exception of some organizations, we are not there yet.
- At the end of the day, it's about doing what's needed without fanfare or glory.

9

Don't Talk Like a B@#$%

When women leaders take tough decisions or actions, they are often viewed differently, given the 'likeability conundrum' where in general, women are expected to be agreeable, warm and nurturing.

I asked some leaders, male and female, how women are perceived when they are very assertive and direct at the workplace. These are some reactions they shared:

- She is being 'aggressive'
- She is being 'very bossy'
- She is a 'tough iron lady'
- She is too 'emotional and is overreacting'
- She is a 'B@#$%'

These perceptions often get compounded in patriarchal cultures. The point may be communicated differently, but the gist remains the same: If a woman conveys a tough message, it is less acceptable than when a man does.

Broadly speaking, when women leaders are perceived as 'too powerful', it threatens to lower their likeability quotient.

In this regard, HR leader and growth mindset advocate Dr Susan P. Chen's viewpoint is relevant: 'Generally speaking, a very outspoken woman is perceived more as a rebel, compared to an outspoken man. And I've seen that across the different countries I have worked in, whether it's a mature market or an emerging one. For instance, it's less prevalent in countries like Norway, but in some countries in Southeast Asia, an outspoken woman is often labelled as a "rebel" or "aggressive" compared to a man who is "confident". This does influence the way women think about engaging or influencing in a leadership role.'

Leaders, both men and women, want to be liked by their teams. For women who are scrutinized more deeply for a range of reasons, this assumes more complexity. How do women leaders navigate this conundrum? How are they perceived and how do they work around this? These are some aspects explored in this chapter.

Here are some strategies and behaviours women leaders have adopted to navigate this tricky terrain.

Tough love

Given that being tough in the land of smiles isn't easy, I asked Lynette how she conveys tough messages in the Philippines in a manner that doesn't antagonize or alienate her colleagues.

Lynette shares her approach here:

> It is difficult to find the balance, but the way I conduct myself is to always assume a position of equanimity. As long as I make sense and am sensitive to the people around me, I don't bother too much or overthink about being liked. I am generally mindful of my words given that Filipinos are sensitive and emotional.
>
> For example, during performance discussions, I make sure that my feedback is always honest but balanced. I think for women it takes a lot to be blunt, mainly because they don't want to come off as being bullcrap. But it's such a sexist thing—the minute women are a bit more aggressive, assertive or blunt, people mutter under their breath, and you can see what they are thinking. This is the balance that you need to strike—you could be tiptoeing over the issues and teetering over the edge and what may be needed is a decisive action or blunt force. Depending on the situation, sometimes if you tiptoe on the edge too much, you won't get the desired outcome because the people you are speaking with may want a direct, no-nonsense approach.

Lynette's approach is to be direct and decisive when needed without overthinking it. Yet, she is cognizant of the words and the tone she uses, given the importance of sensitivity, as discussed in an earlier chapter. She is mindful of getting this balance right and maintains a calm demeanour. The reader will recall her early days in New York, where she learnt to develop a thick skin.

Bindaas or badass?

A recent article in an Indian online portal was titled 'If your boss is tough but fair, work for him'. While reading it, I wondered if by changing one word in this title—so it read 'If your boss is tough but fair, work for *her*'—the article would be equally palatable.

> In Hindu mythology, Goddess Durga epitomizes strength and the victory of good over evil. She is fierce but kind, invincible and right. And while her power and strength are celebrated, with a nine-day festival in her honour, not many Indian women leaders are revered for their power and authority in corporate India. Women leaders seldom challenge or disagree publicly, and they aren't usually aggressive. The Indian leadership model tends to be alpha-male and hierarchical, where the leader is expected to be directive and in charge.
>
> Which is probably why in the past, women who have made it to leadership positions have been gentler in their approach than their male counterparts, although this is changing amongst the younger generation.

In this context, Punita Kumar-Sinha observes from her experience that in the West, typically people who take initiative and speak up do well whereas Indian culture has traditionally rewarded women for being more consensus-building, less aggressive and more self-effacing.

She makes a great point: *Different cultures reward different types of behaviours.*

Another factor that determines communication styles is the profession. For example, women doctors and entrepreneurs in India are fairly assertive. Punita observes that in a setting where hierarchy and going up the ranks is important, women in India fit in and adapt to this. But when women operate in non-linear fields such as in the entrepreneurial, legal, political and medical professions, they are as assertive, or more as women anywhere else.

Coming back to the subject of women in the corporate world, the pitfall when women behave tough or *bindaas,* a Hindi word that means carefree and daring, is that it can come across as unnatural or haughty. Shahrukh Marfatia, a board director and advisor based in Singapore, has mentored several senior leaders and makes this observation: 'Often, I find that both Asian and non-Asian women leaders try to sometimes overcompensate their more natural, caring, self-effacing, humble, serving leadership styles with aggression to match some of their alpha male colleagues or bosses.' This view is broadly corroborated by other leaders, male and female.

The bigger point being made is that tough messages need to be communicated authentically. Pavitra shares how she does this:

> If the tough assertive style is the woman leader's natural style, so be it. But if this behaviour is not authentic, people can see through it. Women don't need to use the same language that men do; they do not need to thump their feet or call it out loudly. They can give a tough message in their own way.
>
> I have used different approaches to deliver direct messages based on the context—it could be healthy humour at times or a straight-to-the-point message when required. In my experience, humour helps to break the ice or diffuse a tense situation; it helps the message land better and is remembered for a long time. Of course, humour needs to be used in a way that's respectful and not seen as frivolous. Whatever the approach, I make it a point to communicate that I should not be taken for granted; there is a line which is important to respect.
>
> I am conscious that as a female leader, by default, people notice how you deal with things and that how you respond can be a big learning and inspiration to others down the line.

Often, in situations like the above, it's more about how something is done, and how authentic it is.

Pavitra makes the point that there is a line, which is important to draw and respect. This is relevant in the Indian context, where exercising power and authority is almost necessary to get work done. And while it is necessary for a leader to convey a degree of authority and decisiveness, he or she needs to be cognizant of striking a balance between the nuances of hierarchy and empathy at the workplace.

Pavitra's observation that women leaders are noticed more certainly strikes a chord. If one looks at countries in Southeast Asia such as Thailand as an example, women may not publicly disagree often, but in all likelihood, there are enough women in the room to make a case or get their point across. They have strength in numbers, which is not always the case in other places and would likely result in a woman's decisions and actions being scrutinized more closely.

Being cognizant of 'face'

'Face' is an important nuance, and working in Asia, one needs to be cognizant of how egos can be bruised and bridges burnt. Polly Ng narrates an anecdote that highlights this aspect:

> I recall an incident with my South Korean head of business some years ago. The business was not doing well, and I spoke with him in an aggressive tone. Later he told me, 'Polly, you are the first woman to talk to me like this.'
>
> If I reflect back, I showed my strength and aggression, but this doesn't work, especially in a male-dominated society. It doesn't motivate the people there. What is fundamental as a

leader is to help your people resolve the problem, but if the men don't ask for help, you have to recognize this and work with them together and ensure that they retain a good face.

> As illustrated in this example, in situations where male colleagues are not comfortable with direct and aggressive communication by women, women leaders need to recognize and resolve the underlying discomfort and tension.
>
> If people need more space or patience because of the prevalent cultural norms, one needs to respect that, especially given the concept of 'face', which is pronounced in Asia. Polly's approach indicates a level of maturity and perceptiveness in understanding and resolving matters like this.

Direct or not?

Being tough involves being direct. What happens when the overarching culture isn't conducive to such direct messages? It's a double whammy from a culture and gender standpoint!

When a dynamic Singaporean leader began working for a European MNC in Asia, she was told that her communication style was quite sharp and direct. This approach worked well in the American organization she had worked in for ten years. But her style was perceived as being too direct in the new Anglo-British organization, and she was advised to tone it down.

Another example is of an Indian leader who after moving to India from the US, had to learn to smoothen the rough edges. Technically sound and analytically driven, she was more focused on the problem-solving aspects of her work. When she moved to India, she was given feedback that she needed to work on her people-related skills. And so, she began paying closer attention to aspects such as building in empathy in her communication style.

Both leaders were advised to tone down their direct approach in order to be in alignment with and more effective in the respective cultures, whether organizational or national.

This is not to say that people have to walk on eggshells. In cultures and organizations that value directness, there is no substitute for straight talk. But in certain situations and contexts, direct messages work better if they are toned down a bit. This probably enables both the message and the messenger to be more palatable.

Sunsanee puts it well:

> As to women giving tough messages, I think that in any culture, men feel threatened a bit or taken aback when the boss is female and a bit aggressive. But there's always a place and time for directness. As leaders, you have to be direct enough with people to know where you're coming from or where you want to go. If you're not direct, people go around in circles, and the organization does not move forward.
>
> I am very direct without being impolite, without being rude and without being overly aggressive. This idea of managing and balancing within the Asian culture is important.

The yin and yang of it

Gregory Rastello, a talent development professional who was based in China for a long time, gives the outside-in view, saying, 'In China, sometimes we see women entrepreneurs who have very strong "yang". In Taoism, yang is masculine, and yin is feminine. These entrepreneurs are often more aggressive and result-driven than women and men working in MNCs.'

This has a parallel with the Indian context, where aggression is nuanced depending on profession, amongst other things. However, in China, while there is ambition and drive, the overarching culture seems to be more veiled, as publisher and author Xu Ge Fei says:

> In the manner of expressing everything, Chinese women are not aggressive. You have the core and the form. In the form, you rarely see Chinese women communicating aggressively. In the core, of course, there is ambition and drive, and you have to be hard but 'hard-softly'. Always.

In this context, Adele, who heads LIXIL in China, discusses her leadership style and way of working as follows:

> A female leader can be better at being compassionate, but she can also be tough. If my team members make mistakes, I get upset, and I express this to them. I don't criticize people all the time, but for some important things, I do it directly, I don't save their face.
>
> But I need to work on how people can better accept what I'm saying. An area that I need to work on is patience. I often use other ways to soften the relationship. I explain to people concerned the reason and purpose of what I'm saying.
>
> People accept my tough messages because they know I am working for the organization or the team, not for myself. So in the end, they see the benefit and the bigger picture. I don't worry about short-term relationships or short-term criticism.

Adele does not shy away from communicating a tough message. Like other leaders, while the message or the 'what' is communicated, she works on 'how' it is conveyed.

Tough messages are about trust. One senior Asian leader told me 'If I ask my employee to go to hell, they will go to hell. Do you know why? Because they trust that after going to hell, they will go to heaven.'

When employees trust that the leader has taken difficult decisions for everyone's benefit in the long term, they are taken in the right spirit. Often, when women leaders use tough language, it is accepted because they have earned the right to do so. As Rohini says, 'Being able to give tough messages becomes easier when you've established some degree of trust. It's like a bank account deposit, which you can draw on. But this takes investment, both by men and women.'

Xu Ge Fei's words 'hard-softly' are a succinct description of the communication style adopted by women leaders, across geographies. From all accounts, women leaders from different industries and countries have one thing in common: they are mindful of striking a balance between direct and indirect, decisive and soft. That seems to be the essence of how women leaders communicate in the Asian context.

The message and the messenger

Bonita Lee talks of her learnings as she communicates messages, including tough and direct ones, across cultures:

> The expectation that women should fit in a frame as a mother and wife is relatively less pronounced in Singapore, and I have not had to flex my style too much; I'm naturally more direct and that fits the local environment. Corporate culture

also defines what is acceptable and can greatly enable how messages are communicated.

In some cultures, tough messages conveyed by women are less accepted. There is an old saying that actions may be tough, but the method should be soft. There is a lot of wisdom in this. The way hard messages are communicated has a strong bearing on how they will be received ... Getting the right people to deliver the messages is equally important to have the best impact.

Another woman leader, Martha,[53] who works in the region has a similar perspective. Before she communicates important messages, she considers, 'What do I want to achieve, and should I always be the one up front?' Over time, she has realized that she is not equally effective in different contexts, and sometimes she has to find the right messenger.

Working across cultures, leaders like Bonita recognize the need to have a range of styles and voices to be effective. There is a time to lead the conversation, and a time to stay back and let someone else be in the driver's seat.

Soft as a marshmallow

When I give feedback, one of my techniques is that I use very direct words, but since I speak softly compared to other women leaders, people don't realize that I'm saying tough things. Everyone says my words are super straight but they are covered in marshmallow. When they absorb my words, they understand what I really mean.

The above account is of how Himari, a Japanese leader in a financial organisation, describes her style of communicating difficult messages in Japan.

---

53 Name changed to protect privacy

Women Leaders in Japan: A Perspective

Shojiro Mitsuzawa, CFO of a healthcare technology start-up in Japan, provides his perspective on Japanese women leaders.

According to him, there are 'two types' of leadership amongst women leaders in Japan: one is an empathetic leadership style and the second is along the lines of a strong military leadership, which is not popular.

The first category of empathetic women leaders are very capable women who can unite members around a single idea and build cooperative relationships. They are good at listening to and incorporating the opinions of people in different positions. The second category comprises men too, but mostly women who are in management positions for the first time.

Shojiro's perception, shared by others, is that when a woman assumes a management position for the first time, she faces perceptions on whether 'she is ready for this position'. This makes her more forceful than necessary, as she tries to exert her power and control over her colleagues, which sometimes leads to failure.

There seems to be a dichotomy where at one level, Japanese women are resilient and restrained; yet those who have prioritized their career can also be vocal, fierce and territorial.

Traditionally in Japanese companies, female colleagues, called *onnanoko*, would serve tea or provide administrative support. Practices such as this, reflective of the broader attitudes to working women in Japan, have probably resulted in women leaders adopting tough outward behaviours in order to be taken seriously. But this seems to be changing slowly.

We discussed how Himari manifests a softer brand of leadership, which is increasingly more prevalent amongst the younger Japanese women leaders. This is summed up by Yagi when he observes: 'Over time a new type of successful female leader has emerged. They demonstrate their capability naturally without drawing too much attention to say, *"I'm here, I'm a female."*'

Getting it right

There are perils of being direct as a Thai leader discovered the hard way. In her words:

> In case of a conflict, I communicate directly and honestly as to how things are working or not working. It doesn't always work because in the Asian context, people are afraid to speak up. And when I tell people that this is how it could be done, I put fear into the space. I have made a lot of people upset after giving them direct feedback.
>
> Over the years, I have toned down the directness and become a little more indirect. I realized I should practice not to be open and honest about everything. As a leader, one can do more of listening and sensing. If people need more space because of the cultural norms, then I need to respect that and give them that and can't keep pushing for people to be more 'Western'.

In this chapter, we have discussed how nuanced communication is, and can be, in the Asian context. The 'how' of conveying the message is important; let's discuss some ways to get this right:

- Being cognizant of the 'how' involves making the effort to frame the message appropriately. As a leader points out, one needs to find a way to deliver a not-so-happy message in a way that people can accept. Often our head is so full of 'this is what I need to accomplish, this is what I need to convey', that we don't spend enough time thinking about who the audience is, what their context is, or how they could accept the message better. Taking the time to frame the message makes a big difference.

- While women leaders may be transparent, they don't necessarily 'need to be open about everything'. They should be cognizant of using their words carefully.
- When managers and leaders call out something as soon as they notice it, the performance management conversation is a shorter one!
- A framework that leaders use to have difficult conversations is a variation of the What-What-Why framework. This entails asking questions on the lines of 'What did you do?' 'What was the outcome?' 'Why is that important?'

  Since this line of questioning helps to focus more on the actions and not as much on the person, it enables a degree of objectivity while delving deeper and strategizing on the way forward.
- Given that nurturing is a celebrated trait amongst women leaders, communicating tough messages in a way that affirms the person's best interests at heart seems to be a winning approach.

  Abanti shares how she has been told that she can land the hardest messages 'like a knife cutting through butter'. Abanti clarifies that while she doesn't couch the message, she tries to ensure that the person leaves with his or her dignity maintained, knowing that it was in the interest

of the business—and often his/her own professional advancement—which ultimately had to carry.
- Lastly, being authentic is key, especially when communicating tough messages. In the example above, Himari is quite direct but because of her appearance or because of the way that she speaks, it sounds deceptively soft. Despite expectations that leaders must be tough, Himari has devised a style that is reflective of her true self.

As seen in this chapter, there's a range in the behaviour of successful women in Asia. There are women leaders who are soft-spoken who do very well, and there are women leaders who are not soft-spoken who also do very well. They have taken the cultural norms and expectations in their stride with maturity and grace and devised an approach that works for them. With experience, they know when to push and when to lean back, when to desist and when to up the ante.

Not every successful woman leader in Asia is patient, empathetic and polite to a fault. If they are good at their job, they are respected. But the ones who have these more palatable qualities are arguably more popular or better liked.

Working women in Asia tend to have a thick skin. They are scrutinized and often attacked from all quarters. If they are aggressive or forceful, they are often perceived to be a B@#$% because it goes against the way men and women are programmed. Whether women leaders are tough in their words or actions, they need to be, first and foremost, mentally tough.

10

Reach and Resilience

I was the first woman pilot to be selected by Air India in the year 1988.

I went to Hisar in Haryana for my private pilot licence. I was the only woman; there was no accommodation or facilities for women at the flying club. The house I was staying in was far away from the flying club. My daily commute on my moped was long and unsafe, and the roads would be deserted. That was the early 80s when there was no way to connect with the family in case I got stuck somewhere. I would constantly keep chanting prayers all the way. I come from a spiritual family, and I have always believed that my power and strength come from the Almighty. In fact, I used to sleep with a knife under my pillow. It was tough, but I managed as I was brought up in an environment where there was no difference between a boy and a girl.

My spirituality has kept me grounded and helped me deal with the highs and lows in life. I believe in the purity and the niceness of people, that we come together for a reason and a purpose. I believe in Pure Soul Quotient (PSQ) as a fundamental need for business ethics and serving the world

I meditate with my team frequently, which keeps us focused, calm and energized. In that state of mind, people come out with better ideas and solutions, because they're in a different space. But you need to do it frequently enough because people tend to go back to their old selves. I encourage my executive team to practise mindfulness. And before I start the meeting, I ask them, 'Let's start with what was the best thing that happened to you yesterday.'

I don't consider I'm working for Air India, I just think I'm working for God, this is my role in this world's drama. That way you don't get affected by the ups and downs; you just take them as part of life, you enjoy your work, you keep giving your best.

Dr Harpreet A. De Singh's account above is a story of reach and resilience. She aspired for the skies, quite literally, and weathered many a storm before being selected as the first woman pilot by India's national airline. However, due to medical reasons, she didn't continue flying. Nonetheless, her journey is trailblazing, in that India today has the highest percentage of female pilots globally.[54]

Dr Harpreet was the first woman CEO of an airline in India-Alliance Air. Her leadership mantra, pun intended, is largely anchored in the power of spirituality.

In this chapter, we discuss how leaders explore new horizons and sustain their drive. They set a high bar and constantly seek to add value to themselves and others. A leader who consciously does this is Kumi Ito, as elaborated below.

---

54 Ragini Saxena, 'At 12.4 per cent, India has twice the number of female pilots as the US', *Business Standard*, 9 August 2022

Exploring new frontiers

> An executive search person asked me to list my top priorities, thinking my list would include position, money and rewards. He was surprised when I told him that it was none of these.
>
> Before the pandemic, I would often meet my friends in the industry for dinner to learn what the new trends and challenges were—this is part of my top priorities. I love new things—new challenges, new solutions, new industries, new approaches, new people. I think I am curious like George the monkey! In a start-up, there are new troubles, new errors and new scope, which is tough, but fun and one can learn a lot.

Kumi's description of being curious like George is such a refreshing descriptor! From the above, it is clear that she appreciates the need to keep abreast of changes and developments in order to grow professionally as well as personally.

The desire to keep learning enables leaders to stay relevant and agile. Another leader who goes looking for new ideas is Mimee, the CEO and co-founder of Techsauce in Thailand, a leading tech knowledge-sharing platform that combines technology content with the world of business and innovation. Mimee shares:

> I started my own company in 2012 with a friend. I believe that ideas are cheap; people can have the same idea, but the key success factor is how we can turn the idea into action. I love a quote of Steve Jobs: 'We cannot connect the dots looking forward, we can only connect the dots looking backward.' We have to trust all the dots will somehow connect in our future, so anyone who has new ideas should dare to act, start small and move fast. I allocate 30 per cent of my time per week to explore new business models and opportunities. I have the confidence to move out of my comfort zone and try new things. My staff thinks of me as a coach and visionary who loves to find new opportunities.

Mimee is recognized as one of the pioneers in building the Thai start-up ecosystem. Her ability to connect the dots and her positive growth mindset have brought her to where she is today. To share a fun fact, she is passionate about food blogging!

Learn and unlearn

Both Kumi and Mimee recognize that people can stagnate if they don't consciously push themselves to explore new things. Dynamic leaders keep a lookout for new trends and views. I know of a leader who makes it a point to meet a person from a different industry every month to understand how the developments in that space can be applied to his industry. That's an example of 'thought leadership' in the literal sense!

For Karishma R. Phatarphekar, partner and tax controversy management leader at Deloitte India, a big part of her professional journey has been about learning, unlearning and relearning. She shares some insights she lives by:

> I learn from failures and mistakes and don't let the fear of failure discourage my team members from trying something new. Debriefing in one's mind and discussing with my mentor why something went wrong is the first step to understanding what went wrong. For instance, when I lost a project with a long-standing client with whom I had a good working relationship for several years, I could not figure out the reason for this. On reflecting, I realized that due to my long-standing relationship with the client, I assumed that I would have won this project as well. I failed to specifically explain the credentials we carried for this specific project. Perhaps I should have communicated with the client more proactively than I did. I learnt you should never assume things or take things for granted. Once I understand what went wrong, I am mindful not to repeat the same mistakes.

Unlearning as you move ahead is super critical. I can give an example here of unlearning that helped me in my career. When I moved up to the position of a manager from an executive, initially I continued doing the grunt work myself. Over time, I realized this focus on administrative duties and checking the boxes impacted the quality and time of deliverables. I needed to improve the art of delegation and unlearn old habits.

Another recent example was when we moved to working from home, in courts that were virtual. As a counsel, I was used to printing everything, making my written notes and marking on papers. When we moved to a virtual way of working, I had to stop printing everything in physical form and use digital tools to mark, reference and tag cases. Over the last two years, I have gotten so used to the digital way of working that I wonder how I was wasting so much paper earlier. This unlearning has not only enabled me to be a tech-savvy lawyer, but I can now appreciate that the grass is indeed greener on the other side!

Reflecting where one went wrong and learning from mistakes is invaluable. Leaders like Karishma recognize this attitude is key to growing both as a leader and as a person.

Good leaders seek to be better versions of themselves. While being aware of their strengths and gaps, these leaders work to acquire new skills. Easier said than done, of course, as one takes on different roles. As Nayantara Bali discovered, when she became a director in an industry she wasn't familiar with. She had to learn and unlearn things as she shares here:

Whether it was developing connections or asking the right questions, I had to develop a new set of skills. I was learning to ask the right questions in the right way. As a director, you have to resist the temptation to comment on operations. You need to stick in your lane. Of course, you can ask a question and let people 'think about it'. As a director, asking the right question in the right way without being overpowering and providing direction is an important skill.

Leaders, including the ones I spoke with, surround themselves with people they can learn from. Speaking of learning from people, someone who does it well and consistently is Roshni Nadar Malhotra. As one of the youngest chairpersons in India, Roshni tries to be up to speed by listening and learning from different people. In her words: 'I learn something new every day. I love the fact that I am challenged every day, which pushes me to learn more.'

> On a slightly unrelated note, one common observation shared by the male leaders I spoke with across China, India and the Philippines is that women take constructive feedback well. They are cognizant of their strengths and the areas they need to work on. And they reflect based on the feedback they get from peers and psychometric assessments. I found it interesting to note how some Chinese, Singaporean and Filipino leaders I spoke with often referred to findings of psychometric tests to illustrate their leadership style. They presented this as a valid data point, unlike others who lean more on a subjective interpretation of their leadership styles.
>
> Successful leaders conduct a personal audit of their leadership; they seek inputs from people who know them in different roles and capacities on the lines of 'how do you see me as a leader?' and 'what can I do better or differently?' This helps them understand how they are perceived and what can be worked on, going forward.

Taking that leap

How often have we heard that 'the magic happens when we go outside our comfort zone?' There is no denying that taking on new interests and projects can be enriching. But as Andy Molinsky points out in his book *Reach*, 'The overall lesson is to pick one's spots. Stay in your comfort zone in certain situations, move slightly outside in others and sometimes, when the circumstances are right, take that big leap.'[55]

Karen Tay Koh, independent non-executive director on the boards of several companies, is a great example of taking that leap. Here she talks about some factors that facilitated her success and a few things that she did differently:

> I've had a diverse career, with some unconventional choices. I believe you have to make your own path because there is no playbook. As the saying goes: 'Luck favours the prepared.' In life when opportunity presents itself, when a door opens from above, you need the mental fortitude to step up to it.
>
> I say this because I took a lot of career risks. For example, after ten years of working as a government official in Asia, I made the cut to study at Harvard University in the US. It was unbelievable that with three young children, I went to graduate school, with no house help. Frankly, it was more my husband's idea, and we just took off and stayed away for five years. 'Luck' threw me an opportunity and I didn't say 'no'.
>
> Another example was of moving to healthcare in 2001. After nineteen years in government finance, joining a

---

[55] Andy Molinksy, Reach: A New Strategy to Help You Step Outside Your Comfort Zone, Rise to the Challenge and Build Confidence, Avery, 24 January 2017

sovereign wealth fund would have been a logical move. But a healthcare posting came up, and I took it on. And after being in public healthcare for seven years, I decided to leave because I wanted to work in the region. On the third day after leaving, I was on a plane to Thailand to work as an advisor to a Thai hospital. Several years later, I went to work in Myanmar, where I had my first experience at a private equity firm, as well as at a local Myanmar hospital.

What enabled my success is the ability and the willingness to take risks and embrace the unknown. Although I enjoy the challenges and the sense of adventure, it's natural to feel anxious. But when the breaks come, you have to take that leap of faith, especially when heaven opens the door for you.

Karen's story is interesting given that women leaders are often perceived to be risk-averse, which is a 'dangerous stereotype' according to Shahrukh Marfatia, an advisor and mentor based in Singapore. Notwithstanding the perceptions or stereotypes, the reality is that women leaders do take risks that are calculated and well thought out. As they feel comfortable, they venture forth beyond the limits set by others and in many cases, themselves. They recognize that, as Andy highlights in *Reach*, the magic can happen both inside and just outside one's comfort zone!

Global mobility and mindset

While many women leaders accept challenging roles that may be outside their comfort zone, they often draw the line at international assignments. This is where the rubber meets the road not just for women but men too, who don't want to leave their homes and countries for a variety of reasons. Within this set, women tend to pass up more opportunities because of societal factors and family responsibilities.

An HR director of an organization in Thailand observes: 'As women progress in their career, you have to go international but many female leaders in Thailand would say that "I'm happy with my career at this point; I don't want to aim higher." Although the woman may be earning more than the husband, she would defer to the family situation and preferences.' That said, in general, Thais are not very 'portable' when it relates to taking up international assignments.

On the other end of the spectrum are the Filipinos. Remittances from overseas family workers, the majority of whom are caregivers such as nurses, domestic helpers and service providers, constitute a significant portion of the country's gross domestic product.

A large number of these overseas family workers (or OFWs as they are referred to) are women who are the primary breadwinners in their families. This is culturally accepted, which is why Filipina women don't face stigmas in going abroad to work, leaving behind their husbands and young children. There is a stoicism in the way my Filipino helper in Singapore works and sends money home every month, taking comfort in the knowledge that her children are looked after by their grandparents.

Given the comfort and conveniences that Singapore offers, Singaporeans are often hesitant to move outside Singapore. Susan Chen, who has worked in both Singapore and Indonesia, makes an interesting point:

> Women in Singapore are ambitious but for reasons like convenience, infrastructure and children's education, they don't accept international stints as much. I found that in both Singapore and Indonesia, women would not take up overseas assignments because of family reasons. So irrespective of the differences across countries in terms of infrastructure or economy, the final expectations of women and their roles still transcend the country perspective.

The reality is that women in general have greater family responsibilities to handle than their male counterparts, which restricts their mobility in terms of taking up assignments across countries. The tendency is often to not rock the boat. Although these are fewer, there are instances where women leaders have accepted international assignments that have worked out well.

On a related note, Bonita Lee, who works in a regional role, shares how an open mind and risk-taking mindset helped her:

> As an early leader, I had a great manager who opened up my mind to 'what's possible'.
>
> So, I tried things that were different and learnt in the process; I put up my hand for projects and work experiences across Southeast Asian markets when many of my peers were seeking experiences 'in the West'. I also took on a few less attractive assignments to learn. My leadership style is a culmination of learning from my successes and failures; taking some risks with myself and sometimes relying mostly on a belief in what is possible.

Looking back, women often say how they didn't have a well-thought-out career plan but what they did right was to follow the opportunity, when it presented itself. Many of the leaders I spoke with did just that. They went through that door and said 'yes' even if it made them uncomfortable initially. Like Bonita, the choices they made and the decisions they took had a positive impact on their career trajectory.

Envisioning goals

Related to the discussion on exploring new opportunities and ideas is another leadership prerequisite, which is being a visionary.

Adele Tao strongly believes that a great leader must be able to translate the company's strategy and share the vision so that people understand their picture of the future and are willing to work for them. Another leader in China, Lilian Wu, points out that envisioning goals and thinking holistically are integral for leaders to be successful in China. According to her, 'Just like a big brother or sister in a traditional family needs to put the family's interest as the priority to sustain the family fortune, the same is true for leaders in China. Whether they are state-owned, local entrepreneur or foreign MNC and whether man or woman, they need to have a holistic view and put the group's interest over the person and team. In general, this mindset is appreciated and respected in China.'

While being visionary is a universal leadership attribute, it seems to be particularly important in China; perhaps a factor of China's long history and legacy of dynasties and rulers.

WHAT'S IN HER BAG: TOOLS TO GROW

What women could do more of

> Interestingly, a few male leaders who have worked in East and Southeast Asia felt that they didn't come across many visionary female leaders in this part of the world. As Jon E. Kaplan says, 'With the exception of a few individuals and organizations, female leaders at some point become more figureheads and more of relationship managers,'
>
> In a similar vein, Yagi, a successful leader in Japan, feels that at senior levels, women sometimes tend to lack a dynamic view of business. A strong believer in women's leadership abilities, he advises women leaders to develop a wider view of business and the environment, beyond their jobs.
>
> To update and upgrade business intelligence and keep learning is a point worth taking note of. And while Yagi's advice is relevant for both genders, women do tend to get stuck in the nitty-gritty of their professional and personal lives a bit more. Women leaders would do well to make their own learning and growth a priority. As leaders, staying relevant is key as one grows in the organization.

Resilience

If there is one trait that is fairly evident across Asia, it would be resilience. This is probably a factor of the developing and emerging world, where success with its trappings and material comforts is aspired to, encouraged and coveted. Working hard and making personal sacrifices is accepted and celebrated in corporate boardrooms and hawker stalls alike.

At one level, resilience is the ability to adapt to changes, at another level it is the capacity to face adversity and endure hardship, which varies across countries and people. Resilience is about being tenacious in the face of difficulties and recovering quickly from them.

A value that is prevalent in Japanese society is *gaman*, which is manifested in the way the Japanese deal with challenging situations without complaining. Whether it's the pain of hunger or a difficult boss, they hide their discomfort and anguish. As Yurika Kurakata points out, *gaman* can strengthen resilience but is also an acknowledgement or tacit acceptance that things aren't going to change soon.

I have seen the destruction of houses and loss of lives caused by typhoons in the Philippines, and what is amazing is how quickly people bounce back and begin the process of building up. Rarely complaining, they take things in their stride and smile to face another day.

One observation is that women seem to emerge stronger from tragedies and losses; there are countless stories of how women turned desperate situations and losses into exemplary success stories, sometimes with no real business or corporate experience.

Attributes such as resilience are increasingly associated with present-day successful leadership. According to a relevant article on fostering women leaders,[56] some of the most important capabilities that leaders need are resilience, grit and confidence. Resilience allows us to get up after making a mistake or encountering a challenge, grit allows us to push through walls and rise above challenges, and confidence helps transform challenging experiences into greater self-assurance, not self-doubt.

---

56 Lareina Yee, 'Fostering women leaders: A fitness test for your top team', *McKinsey Quarterly*, January 2015.

Taking risks requires courage and resilience. As Karen says, one needs to take that leap of faith. This reference to faith and belief in a higher power is a source of strength and energy for leaders, especially in an uncertain, volatile world. In this regard, the reader will recall Dr Harpreet Singh's journey earlier in this chapter.

Given the dynamic nature of current business environments, leaders need to learn from the past, envision the future, and navigate the changes of the present. To be comfortable with discomfort is both a necessity and a need.

The ability to be focused, embrace risks with fortitude and agility are all key requisites in today's world. It's about keeping a cool head and staying positive despite changes and challenges.

I have seen successful leaders take both success and failure in their stride and learn as much from success as they do from failure. These leaders show us that instead of looking externally, how can we turn the spotlight on ourselves focusing on our work and our strengths.

I'd like to end this chapter on a personal note. The past two years have been a period of upheaval for me. A creative pursuit involves giving shape to a blank slate (or paper in this case), which requires a great deal of inner resolve, discipline and commitment. There were days when I didn't think I had it in me to do anything constructive, much less write a book. But what carried me through was my passion for writing and the belief that someone up there had my back. In the process, I learnt a few things about reach and resilience.

Regardless of our struggles, we all have that inner power and strength; it needs to be tapped into and channelled.

They said

- If you don't have a clear vision of what your short, medium and long-term priorities are, you will never be a good decision-maker.
- Change makers are people with one foot outside where you're able to see the vision and the future of what you want to create and the change that you want to make. But you have one foot inside, which means that you can also relate to why things are the way they are and be able to be that bridge. So sometimes that tension can be difficult when you are navigating both worlds of transition.

11

How They Lead

As I spoke with people while conducting research for this book, I realized that there are plenty of women stars in the Asian galaxy. Bold, bright and beautiful, they radiate energy and warmth.

Drawing from eighteen months of research and conversations with a wide spectrum of women leaders, there are some leadership attributes that are commonly manifested. Let's explore what these are and how women lead in this part of the world.

Do women lead differently from men?

Speaking of how women lead, there do seem to be some traits that are more gender-specific than others.

One of the people I spoke with likens the difference between a Chinese male leader and a female leader as the difference between the energy of water and that of a mountain. At the risk of generalizing, the differences between the genders may not be as stark but they are prevalent.

As per an HBR study,[57] women were thought to be more effective in 84 per cent of the competencies that we most frequently measure. Women leaders were rated as excelling in taking initiative, acting with resilience, driving for results, and displaying high integrity and honesty. Men were rated as being better on two capabilities: 'develops strategic perspective' and 'technical or professional expertise'.

Men often have a single-minded focus to drive business goals whereas women tend to take into account a range of aspects, not just the immediate issue. In the book *How Women Rise,* the authors Sally Helgesen and Marshall Goldsmith,[58] observe that 'women's attention for the most part operates like radar, scanning the environment, picking up a broad range of clues, and paying attention to context. Whereas men's attention operates more like a laser, focusing tightly and absorbing information in sequence.'

On a related note, a male leader in Thailand, observes that in his experience, women leaders tend to consider the customer's perspective whereas male leaders usually focus on the technical and functionality perspective. A few male managers I spoke with felt that women leaders had a more varied approach, as

---

57 Jack Zenger and Joseph Folkman, 'Women Score Higher Than Men in Most Leadership Skills' *Harvard Business Review, 25 June 2019*

58 Sally Helgesen and Marshall Goldsmith, *How Women Rise: Break The 12 Habits Holding You Back*, Random House, 26 April 2018

opposed to a more stereotypical approach displayed by their male leaders.

In general, women leaders display authority differently from men in the sense that they don't crave power or credit quite as much. Women tend to spend time and effort on tasks, even if these do not directly result in growth or enhancement of their roles.

According to Greg Rastello, women leaders put the team at heart. They play less on competition to motivate employees to stretch and reach their business objectives. In general, women display greater empathy and engagement and are more explicit. Difficult conversations are easier to have with women.

Women are willing to change their stance if needed. As a woman leader observes, 'They don't dig in their heels, even if they are wearing them!' A related point is that while men seek feedback in bullet points, women tend to explore feedback more. For instance, a man may ask, 'Tell me three things so I can do better', whereas a woman may say, 'How could I have handled it better?' 'Where do you think I went wrong?'

Shiv Shivakumar points out that women tend to have a better reading or assessment of a person's personality and character compared to men. He feels that men tend to go a lot by the recency effect whether it is results or interactions, but women are able to provide more insight into a person's character.

While this list isn't exhaustive, it is indicative of the differences in ways of working and leading. As to more definitive metrics on the question of whether women lead differently from men, the data may not be sufficient to draw conclusions. As Shiv points out, 'At present only 8 per cent of CEOs of Fortune 500 companies are women. Only when this number moves substantially higher, reflecting more women in senior management, can one make more accurate inferences as to whether and how women lead differently.'

Leadership expectations

Within the umbrella of Asian leadership, ways of working and leading are manifested differently across the region due to different value systems and expectations. Within the overarching societal and cultural make-up of each country there is a preference for a certain genre of leadership. Capabilities and abilities being a given, both male and female leaders are expected to conform to these norms within a range, making allowances for their personal styles and traits.

For example, in Thailand, the expectation of a leader is heart over head, to put it simplistically. A good leader is approachable and humble.

Thailand is considered a feminine society whereas Japan is considered a masculine one as per Hofstede's cultural dimensions. So, the overarching leadership styles at a country level are different.

Over and above this, women leaders are also viewed through a patriarchal lens with Asian countries placed differently on this metric.

Leadership traits may be universal, but leadership behaviours aren't always perceived the same way. For example, it is commonly accepted that a male leader is aggressive, and a female leader is collaborative. This may be a factor of one's role and function and is prevalent in the Western world too, but in Asia, because of the underlying values, this assumes cultural overtones.

As per a study, men are perceived as confident if they are seen as competent, but for women to be seen as confident, they must come across as both competent and warm.[59]

In the Asian context, does this translate to mean empathetic, nurturing and maternal? Dr Susan P. Chen dissects this well:

> What I find interesting in the Asian context is that there's a socially constructed approach to leadership. If you behave in a way that is aligned to the 'socially acceptable' Asian woman—motherly, emotionally connected—then you are considered as an authentic good leader. But if you behave in a way that is different, such as being aggressive or speaking up to the senior leadership team, you are perceived as 'going against the norm'.
>
> The perception of being a female leader in Asia includes a lot more of that 'socially acceptable' expectation. As a leader, I have felt the pressure of having to manoeuvre both the Asian expectation of being a nurturing leader with my European upbringing and influences.
>
> Also, when it comes to women leaders, there is an expectation to tie their success with the team's success. Female leaders' success is often perceived as collective whereas male leaders' success is seen as more individualistic. This may be because there is a lot more leniency for men to behave and look aggressive and successful. On the other hand, it is innately against the socially constructed narrative of a 'successful' female leader.

In a sense, this expectation is innate to the broader cultural nuances of many Asian countries. We discussed earlier how Thai and Filipino societies are intrinsically more feelings-based with humility, harmony and hierarchy being interwoven

---

[59] Margarita Mayo, 'To Seem Confident, You must be seen as Warm', HBR *Guide for Women at Work*, Harvard Business Review Press 2019

in the ecosystem, so leadership is often an extension of these societal nuances. Women born and raised with these cultural expectations, as it were, have an innate understanding of these norms. Their behaviours at work and outside are a reflection of this understanding and/or acceptance.

A great example of a leader who displays this understanding to effectively work and lead is Renyung Ho. In her words:

> A few years ago someone said to me, 'We can't decide if you are a harmless, nice girl or if you are someone who is actually going to make a difference.' That remark stuck with me.
>
> I may not hear or see biases often but I feel them constantly. I know that I will always be judged. Over time, I've learnt not to take these things personally. I focus on doing my best. I'm one of few females in the senior management/leadership team, and I am younger; I'm learning what it means to navigate that space and claim my sovereignty.
>
> Whether it's the 'Asian' culture or hierarchy, I am a lot more careful and deliberate about my choice of words and how I am, given this is also my second stint in the organization. It's only in the past few years that I have learnt how to express difference in a way that is not combative. I'm actually a very direct person, but since 'face' is super important in an Asian context, I try and create sensitivity. I have learnt to listen, give respect and read the subtext.
>
> The process of carving out my individuality has been about always establishing a shared goal and intention. I want to be someone who builds a good team rather than a top-down leader. If I'm running a meeting, I ensure that everyone attending it has an equal share of voice. I aim to create a shared vision with teams, inspiring people to come along as opposed to being a single person holding the torch. My style is informal, communicative and transparent.
>
> I used to be dressed in a much more bohemian feminine way, now I wear a lot more jackets. I used to wear prints

and a lot of colour; now I wear more of black, white and blue. Although I have toned down my dressing style and my communication style, I get feedback that I'm intimidating. Perhaps it's because I'm also female—is an assertive female leader scarier than an assertive male leader?

> This anecdote touches upon so many themes of this book.
>
> Asia has many family-owned businesses, where decision-making is generally centred around the founder-owner of the business. As a young generation leader in a family business, Renyung is cognizant of how things work and does not want to disrupt the way people are used to working. At the same time, she brings her own stamp and style in the way she conducts meetings, works and interacts with her team.
>
> She accepts that she will face biases and judgement and takes this in her stride. She has toned down her casual, bohemian attitude of her initial days, and having earned credibility, she establishes her individuality in other ways.

Let's move on to discussing some broad ways in which women lead in Asia.

Hard drive and software

An observation based on my chats with leaders and managers in Asia is that successful women in this part of the world display a combination of a hard and soft approach. A tough no-nonsense manner when it comes to deliverables and decisions, but a softer side when it comes to influencing and communicating. Given the Asian context, aren't these traits desirable for men as well? Yes, if men have them, it adds to their 'aura' of being a good leader. For women, more often than not, it is par for the course.

As Polly Ng says, 'I think the women who come to leadership positions, including me, have a combination of masculine characteristics, like being result-oriented, assertive and confident, and deep-rooted feminine characteristics.'

Women leaders manifest both the drive and the compassion. Of Belgian origin, Marie-Therese Claes was based in Asia for twelve years and observes that, 'Southeast Asian women leaders combine a mellow, gentle side with a toughness. They can make tough decisions, take responsibilities and at the same time, take care of their teams.'

This combination gets accentuated or diluted depending on the cultural drivers and societal influences. This style works well particularly in countries such as Thailand, Philippines, Indonesia and India given the broader societal nuances of politeness and respect.

The diagram below from the State of the Heart Report shows some interesting nuances and differences amongst women leaders across regions.

WOMEN LEADERS' GLOBAL COMPARISON

There are regional differences in these balance scales among female senior leaders:

Source: State of the Heart Global Report 2021

It is observed from the above chart that higher emotional self-awareness is consistent for women leaders across regions.

One striking feature is that women leaders in Asia show the lowest propensity for taking risks. This can be partly attributed to their cultural orientation. However, there are countless instances where women courageously push boundaries in their own way. The findings above are also relative since the study extends to the region beyond Southeast Asia. But this is certainly a relevant finding that successful women leaders and those aspiring to be, should be cognizant of.

Leading with 'why'

Let me share a story of two leaders in an organization based in Asia. A dynamic and experienced leader, who led from the front, helmed it. He was clear about the organization's priorities and the goals that everybody needed to achieve, and he was equally clear about 'what was not needed'. By eliminating the noise and clutter, he was able to zero in on the organization's objectives.

He had the capability to take tough decisions, implement strategies. and achieve deliverables. Notwithstanding these abilities, he didn't succeed in the role. The reason? He didn't have the people on board to achieve his vision, he wasn't able to influence and enlist followers. As John Maxwell says, 'He who thinks he leads, but has no followers, is only taking a walk.'

This person was succeeded by Lisa[60], another dynamic and experienced leader who had a different style. Lisa started with the 'why'; she wanted to understand the purpose and the premise of the goals. She didn't operate from the belief that 'she knew best'.

---

60 Name changed for privacy

Her approach was around asking questions and understanding what people needed from her in order to enable success. Lisa empowered people. She would support, guide and inspire the team so that together, they could achieve the impossible.

Lisa's mindset was centred on leading people and not just leading a business. It was about building trust and leading with influence. Her conviction and sense of purpose made people follow her.

The purpose of this anecdote is not to show a dramatic contrast between genders; these attributes are evident in leaders across genders and cultures. That said, women leaders tend to gravitate towards certain facets of leadership.

> If male leaders begin with the 'what', women leaders often begin with the 'why'. They lead with their values and with a strong sense of purpose. Academic studies show that women are more likely to lead through inspiration, transforming people's attitudes and beliefs, and aligning people with meaning and purpose, rather than through carrots and sticks, than men are.[61] Tomas Chamorro Premuzic and Cindy Gallop, '7 Leadership Lessons Men Can Learn from Women,' *Harvard Business Review*, 1 April 202
>
> We have seen how Vanitha, as a regional leader, took a step back to ask about and understand the specific areas in which she could support her country leaders. Renyung and Lilian sought to explore and enhance their teams' alignment with their goals. Women leaders influence with their values, as seen in the way Polly engages with her team of volunteers

---

61 Tomas Chamorro Premuzic and Cindy Gallop, '7 Leadership Lessons Men Can Learn from Women,' *Harvard Business Review*, 1 April 2020

> and younger team members. Rohini inspires her people to follow her not because they need to but because of what she stands for. These leaders are able to connect the dots to paint a broader picture. They lead with humility, and they focus on the value that they can bring and the synergy that they can bring about.

In my conversations with women leaders, I noticed that many of them pay attention to honing their teams' strengths and interests. In a related example, Sofia Shakil, an international development professional with more than twenty-five years' experience with multilateral finance and international organizations, shares how she encourages her colleagues to bring their personal experiences and perspectives to design and enrich their work. As she puts it, 'In any job, it's always about the people you work with at all levels that make the difference. I believe that if you allow them to pursue their passion and draw on their personal experiences, it's so much more meaningful.'

Nurturing and the mom factor

Many of the women I spoke with in Asia mentioned that their inherent nurturing and maternal instincts helped them manage people better. According to Sunsanee, a key part of the leadership style of Asian women is being supportive, guiding their team and inspiring them to work towards the goal. She says that 'Senior female leaders in Asia are perceived more like an older sister rather than an authoritative boss. In Indonesia, I saw that women in senior positions are called *ibu*, a word that also means mother, out of respect. This kind of reference and relationship amongst female leaders is quite unique to Asia.'

A senior leader in a regional role mentioned how her team would always appreciate how protective she was of them and that even when expressing her disappointment, anger or frustration, her team thought she was more maternal as opposed to somebody just chewing them out.

At the risk of generalizing, qualities such as maternal and nurturing are perhaps more prevalent amongst women leaders of the older generation. This is also seen in Karen's observation of her role models from the older generation. She describes Singaporean leaders such as Mrs Christina Ong, founder of the COMO group, and Dato Dr Rosie Tan, Group CEO of Tan Chong Motor Holdings Berhad (TCMH), as being intelligent and successful, never afraid to display their nurturing and caring side.

A related point is that leaders of family businesses tend to be more nurturing. Asia has a large number of family businesses, which often witness an inter-generational transfer of leadership. As loyalty and relationships are key in this kind of business structure, leaders tend to be nurturing, forgiving and at times cranky!

Speaking of being maternal, does motherhood enable women to bring a unique perspective to their leadership role? I was recently on a jury to judge India's best human resources managers under the age of forty. Almost all of the female candidates, and there were a sizeable number, introduced themselves in their professional capacity *and* as mothers. It was a part of their identity that they were proud to embrace, even in a two-minute introduction.

In a sense, this was a reminder of what they stood for and brought to the workplace. My experience of being a mother is that it equips you with some skill sets that can be leveraged to good use, whether it is the ability to resolve conflict or adapt to situations, amongst other things.

This is not to say that people who aren't mothers are inferior or any less equipped. Tiger Mom or not, the mom factor is an additional facet of leadership that is enriching, in a real and relatable way.

Sofia Shakil sums it well when she says: 'I've often felt that in teams that I've managed whether it's at The Asia Foundation or at ADB/World Bank, managing them implies a combination of being a mother, a counsellor and a little bit of a caretaker. I don't know how much of it is natural and how much of it is because of responsibilities/expectations placed on women. You end up developing eyes at the back of your head!'

Leadership with empathy in a changing world

As discussed above, the older generation of leaders had a nurturing and maternal style and were unafraid to show that they cared.

From all accounts, empathy is considered a vital skill set for leaders post the pandemic.

Pavitra Singh points out that 'During Covid, nobody had answers to the situations, but I saw women leaders naturally asking questions, seeking divergent points of view and helping to drive consensus. The silver lining of Covid was that the men are realizing and learning from what the women bring to the table.'

Prime minister of New Zealand Jacinda Ardern's speech during the Covid crisis is an interesting example of how she came across when handling the crisis. Dressed in her pyjamas with her kids around, she got people to see her humanness and simplicity.

I see this easy-going, casual demeanour adopted by younger leaders too. For instance, Renyung has an understated air about her that belies her focus and drive. As a younger generation entrepreneur, Mimee doesn't believe much in hierarchy. Despite being an introverted person, she has an open and transparent way of communicating in the organization. For them, authentic leadership is being themselves quite literally. Their colleagues get what they see and see what they get.

As discussed in the chapter on Results and Relationships, there is a progression of EQ amongst women leaders as they advance in their career.[62] In addition to enhancing their EQ, as women leaders go up the ranks, they also lean towards more emotional self-awareness, greater optimism, higher intrinsic motivation and achieving results through influence.

The 'how' is important: flex and adapt

Leadership is universal but it's also contextual. In the rapidly changing world of today, it's less of 'What is your leadership style?' and more of 'How appropriate is your style, does it fit the situation, the context and the people?'

As Polly points out, the way one leads teams and manages people is context-dependent and culture-related. And at times, it is gender- and generation-related too. Polly elaborates:

> When working with female teams especially younger ones when I established my social venture, Global Women Connect (GWC), I found that the leadership style I have used for twenty years with international companies in a male dominated industry did not influence the same for

---

[62] State of the Heart Global Report 2021

them. When leading big corporate male teams, I established my straight-forward and task-oriented style. But rationally focusing on doing the right things did not always work for the younger female teams.

Through the process, I learned that it is also crucial to take care of and be more understanding of their emotions. Eventually I developed an empathetic leadership style which better encourages and motivates female teams to flourish in their own ways.

The core values and principles stay the same, but to be effective, good leaders adapt their way of working and leading based on the situation, priorities and people. For instance, if Kumi is interacting with someone who is very detail oriented, she can switch from a more intuitive style to using the underlying data. Her ability to adapt to the other person's mood, behaviour and situation helps her respond to situations in the most effective way.

Kumi tweaks her approach in small, unobtrusive ways so as not to ruffle feathers. And in a sense, that seems to be the formula to successfully work and succeed in Japan. Given the importance of conformity to norms, for a female leader to bring about changes, she has to contextualize change and make it palatable for the group.

In other words, she has to make an omelette but not break eggs.

As discussed earlier, in Asia, the 'how' is the operative word when it comes to behaviours, actions and words. Women in Asia portray a more flexible external behaviour in terms of how they interact and get things done while staying true to their core. They adapt without compromising on their values to be effective in a particular context. This may be one feature of 'Asian' leadership.

And women are naturally better at this. There is richness in diversity of experiences, cognitive abilities, points of view and skillsets. And when one is able to connect the different pieces, it adds meaning and value.

Balancing mind, body and soul

The need or the inclination to 'balance' invariably came up in conversations with women managers and leaders in Asia. What was interesting to note was the aspects that were balanced. It wasn't just work and life, home and office.

Senela, who runs an organization called Women Empowered Global, says, 'What has worked for me is a combination of nature, nurture and opportunities. Above all, I have a spiritual belief and connection to everything, including my work that I am doing right now.'

Like Senela, many women leaders derive their strength from their family and faith. Family is their strength and often, spirituality and a belief in a higher power can be their go-to. Of course, this is not unique to women leaders, but it seems to be more present amongst women.

Many of the women I spoke with had developed varied interests outside their work and home. Kumi Ito is a weekend singer. Chris Ng tries to learn a new skill every year, such as piloting a speed boat and learning Muay Thai. Lynette Ortiz works out regularly and tries not to skip her thrice a week regimen. Mimee is passionate about food blogging, and Punita Kumar-Sinha has an interest in Indian dance. Purvi Sheth has a part time culinary business, the proceeds of which she donates to a childcare centre.

These women have found their own ways to grow, reflect and energize. Many volunteer their time and resources to give back to society, and others groom younger leaders in the community. Their varied interests and activities enrich their lives and perhaps sustain their drive.

HOW WOMEN LEAD: IN A NUTSHELL

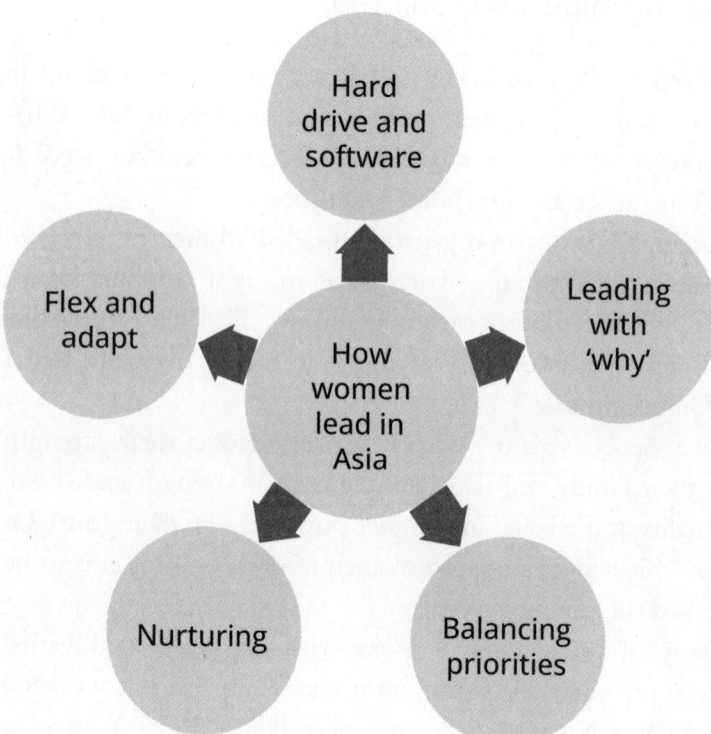

The women leaders I met don't think of themselves as women first, leaders second. They don't play the woman's card. That said, they have some natural traits that they use to their, and others', advantage. Their leadership is a good example of what holistic leadership should be, combining aspects of strength, decisiveness and, at the same time, empathy.

Competence, perseverance and a result-orientation are must-haves. But in a career journey of twenty to thirty years, one needs that inner strength, drive and resilience. For many of the women I spoke with, they considered leadership as a privilege, not a right. It boils down to having competence, character and charisma.

In an anecdote from the non-corporate world, when an Asian female chef was entrusted with managing the kitchen of a fancy restaurant for the first time, she debated whether she should behave demanding and dictatorial like the other senior (male) chefs there. But on reflection, she didn't think this was necessary. She felt that if the leader has the trust and respect of the team and everyone is working towards the same goal, that's what matters.

This encapsulates how women work and lead, whether as head chef or CEO.

Traits across the straits

Being a leader and evolving as one entails developing an appreciation for both the hard and softer aspects of leadership and differentiating between attributes that are a 'need to have' and 'nice to have'.

One can't generalize the attributes that women leaders manifest beyond a point as factors such as position, experience, personality, age, education and organization culture matter. However, based on the research undertaken, these are some attributes that were common to these women leaders:

- They deliver results consistently and take accountability.
- They build a sense of connect and carry their people along.

- They provide context and share information.
- They encourage people to seize opportunities and make tough calls.
- They identify the stakeholders and key influencers and manage their relationships with them.
- They keep the best interests of their team in mind.
- They take calculated risks with the faith that things will work out.
- They dare to push boundaries and disrupt.
- They manage the aggression that alpha male colleagues test them with.
- They are agile and able to work around complexity and change.
- They take cognizance of the bigger picture and adapt—a skill that they learn to use and leverage as they go up the ladder.
- They have a high degree of self-awareness; they know their strengths and their areas for improvement.
- They constantly learn and grow; they reflect on their successes and their failures and course correct when needed.
- Nonchalant about their achievements and success, many shy away from the limelight. They don't whine and complain, they get on with the job.
- They have an arsenal of tools: resilience, grit, equanimity, tact, a sweet voice, a sharp tongue, a long memory or a short temper!

These traits aren't unique to women, but they are certainly prevalent and, in many cases, more pronounced. In a lighter vein, these attributes can be grouped under 'fire and ice'. *Fire* in terms of being on point, results-oriented, having the zest to achieve, being proactive and decisive. *Ice* in terms of being inclusive, collaborative, empathetic, calm and keeping a cool head.

12

More or Less

I asked my interviewees: What should women do more of? What should women do less of?

Based on their inputs, here's the cheat sheet:

- ✓ Build the confidence and ambition to go for the top job.
- ✓ Start small, dream big, but get going.
- ✓ Embrace opportunities to take on operational roles or volunteer for projects that will give you an edge in understanding customers and the day-to-day challenges of running a business.
- ✓ Make the effort to constructively network and build a reputation beyond the day job. In today's world,

networking does not necessarily mean going out for a drink with the boys/girls.
- ✓ Build your brand. Work on building on a core subject matter or specialization that you will be regarded for.
- ✓ It is helpful to be aware of the changes in the external environment. Regularly taking stock of one's career is good.
- ✓ Be courageous to think, say and act. Don't hesitate to share ideas for fear that others have already considered something similar. This fear holds women back from expressing themselves—let it go.
- ✓ Manage your physical and mental energy so you can accomplish your tasks. Build in moments daily for exercise and meditation to be healthy and happy.
- ✓ Stay current and keep learning. Read, learn and interact with people you can grow from.
- ✓ Women are excellent multitaskers; build that into an advantage.
- ✓ Think outside the box.
- ✓ For women who want it all, prioritize and focus on a few areas and do them really well.
- ✓ Find and create your tribe within the company, a like-minded group whether it's women or men.
- ✓ Learn to manage expectations. Aim for less perfection on the home or office front.
- ✓ Recognize that you are super and admit your limitations.
- ✓ At the end of the day, it's about figuring out what your priorities are in life, where you see yourself and how you transition from one phase to the other.

- ✓ Put in place a change management process to balance varied needs and expectations. Consider the impact of a change in job or career on family members and build a communication plan accordingly.
- ✓ Always value yourself. If you don't value yourself, no one else will.
- ✓ Include your family in your career aspirations and enlist their support.
- ✓ Engage with colleagues and build support and awareness for your proposals and ideas before meetings.
- ✓ Say yes to opportunities rather than live with regret.
- ✓ Have less guilt and more confidence.
- ✓ Take a step back and let things be.
- ✓ Don't pretend to be someone you are not.
- ✓ Don't be a 'trophy' CEO.
- ✓ Shed your complexes and false notions such as 'You can't climb up the ladder if you don't dress up, can't network or have kids'.
- ✓ Don't make success and failure bigger than they are.
- ✓ Women often don't feel entitled in board positions—show interest in board roles.
- ✓ Don't coach or mentor women exclusively; women benefit from mentoring men as well.
- ✓ Using the language of men is not necessary to keep up with men.
- ✓ Don't be apologetic about balancing work with family and other priorities

- ✓ Stop overthinking decisions and their fallout.
- ✓ Never ask for something because you are a woman; never ask for a pass.
- ✓ Don't lose your caring and nurturing side.
- ✓ Stand tall and proud. Be bold, bright and brilliant, and above all, celebrate being a woman and own your success!

Conclusion

The world of work has changed dramatically, and the next few years will witness more changes that will impact how women and men work. Going forward, these are some trends that we have seen and will continue to see more of:

- Leadership through influence versus through command and control is a growing trend in organizations of the future.
- There is a need to adapt to the needs and priorities of a dynamic world. For instance, greater resilience, agility and digital skills are relevant now more than ever. In today's world, having knowledge is important, but what's key is how one applies this knowledge to add value and stay relevant.

- There is an unprecedented accent on digitization and increased applications of artificial intelligence (AI). Working from home/virtually has facilitated an openness and flexibility in mindsets and structures. New styles and skills will be needed as people go about establishing trust in diverse contexts and become more effective in working and collaborating in a remote, hybrid world.
- People have become more purpose-driven in their work, they want to have meaning and alignment of values at the workplace. They want to increasingly do what matters to them and contribute in a meaningful way. Employee well-being has emerged as a big area of focus and attention.
- There is a rise in empathetic and transparent leadership. Employees seek an environment where they feel safe to speak up and can challenge the status quo. During the pandemic, women leaders displayed their softer side unabashedly. In the post-pandemic world, they may be better poised to lead with empathy given their cultural and natural inclination to work and lead with these traits. It's relevant to mention here that while women are generally considered as being more empathetic, this quality should not be considered the bastion exclusively of women leaders, especially given that empathy is the trait of the future.
- The need for freedom and flexibility was accentuated during the pandemic for both genders. The desire for autonomy is especially pronounced in the gig economy and amongst millennials. This is possibly a driver of the huge increase in entrepreneurship in the past ten years. Whether it is China, India or any of the other Asian

countries, there are a growing number of women founders and entrepreneurs. There has been a shift in gender roles with women assuming leadership roles outside the house and increasingly, being the sole breadwinners.

- Women leaders are reaching out to younger women to mentor and coach them. More tangible efforts are being made to make women a part of the conversation and decision-making in offices and board rooms.
- The younger generation of women is more focused on their careers and don't feel compelled to marry. In countries such as Thailand and India, expectations around girls getting married by a certain age, or at all, are slowly changing. Older generations are more accepting of the new generation's aspirations and preferences. For instance, Japanese women are beginning to pursue their own agendas. They are postponing or forgoing marriage in record numbers.[63]

An Asian leader remarked in a lighter note: 'These days in several Asian countries, there's less parental pressure on the girls to get married so in another ten years, we will see a lot of women in senior positions. If anything, I worry that the men may fall behind!'

By focusing on women's leadership in this book, the idea is not to dilute the tenets or essence of leadership. Leaders are leaders, regardless of gender, but the reality is that, in many instances, women's backstories and trajectories are different and unique.

---

63 Motoko Rich, 'A Novelist Breaks the Code of Being a Woman in Japan', *The New York Times*, 9 May 2020

CONCLUSION

Cultural and entrenched social norms are intractable obstacles to women's leadership in Asia.[64] Women everywhere face challenges and pressures. That said, this is often amplified in Asia, which is why, although Asia is growing on so many levels, there is a case for enhanced women's leadership in Asia. While celebrating women's success, one needs to recognize that success is not only about acknowledging what is visible. As we are aware, hopefully now more than ever, navigating the journey is more complex because of cultural and societal expectations, which are seldom called out.

This book has been an effort to see women's success against the broader socio-economic landscape and recognize the progress made against this backdrop. Addressing cultural expectations and systemic barriers requires an intervention on various levels. By narrating these examples and stories, the idea is to share how women have made strides and in their own ways impacted their careers and to an extent, their eco system. They have focused on controlling what they can and their success is a testament to this drive and focus. These are hardworking, ambitious women who made it to senior levels.

However, one has also come across women in the real world who pushed their way through and got breaks that weren't deserved. As one has seen play out often enough, if the core in terms of expertise, maturity and leadership is not strong, one can only go so far. These exceptions are not inspiring in my book, pun intended!

---

64 Astrid S. Tuminez, Rising to The Top – A Report on Women's Leadership in Asia, Lee Kuan Yew School of Public Policy, National University of Singapore, 2012

I hope this book serves as a reminder not to get bogged down by how people perceive or pull women down. This requires women to stay the course, make bold choices and in the process, become role models for many others. As more women work and lead, it shouldn't be seen as a loss for men but instead as expanding the pool of talent and a win-win all around. In an ideal world, women leaders would be regarded first and foremost as professionals who bring their calibre and capabilities to the table.

Women may be fewer in number in leadership roles, but they are often society's role models. Even at lower positions in the organisation, a steady job and income earns them a voice in the home and family. I have seen first-hand the contributions and sacrifices a woman makes and the positive difference this makes in her world—workplace and family.

The reality is that even when women have the ambition, education and opportunities, to sustain their drive and trajectory, they need support from their ecosystem. So do men, of course, but for women it can be a game changer. One sees how successful woman leaders from Asia attribute their success to strong pillars in their life, who encouraged and supported them to be the best version of themselves.

We discussed some of the attributes that women bring to the table. Despite the differences across countries, some traits were commonly displayed and manifested. As discussed in the chapter on *How They Lead*, women leaders display a combination of a hard and soft approach. They have a focus on results and connect and care for colleagues and clients. They empower people, leveraging the deeper values and sense of purpose. They connect the dots and paint a broader picture. They flex and adapt their leadership style or communication to best suit the situation, priorities and people.

CONCLUSION

When we speak of women's leadership, the narrative is often around 'what is lacking' or 'what needs to be fixed'. However, women bring so much more to the workplace. They expand the definition and meaning of leadership, bringing in different skills and strategies to lead through influence. They create inclusive workplaces. They look over and beyond. Their approach is multifaceted and enriching on so many levels. Their leadership brings freshness and some much-needed vibrancy. Most importantly, they lead with empathy, they can adapt their style and they find different ways to energize and replenish themselves—key skills in the world of today and tomorrow. Given the trends in the future of work, these attributes of how women work and lead will hold them in good stead.

Ultimately, life is about both logic and magic. Women leaders recognize that and live by it!

Additional References

Chapter 1

- 'Thai Phrases Speaking to older and younger people', *Thailand Breeze*

  http://www.thailandbreeze.com/thai-phrases-speaking-to-older-and-younger-people.html

- 'Confucianism', Resource Library, *National Geographic Society*

  https://education.nationalgeographic.org/resource/confucianism

- Philippines, *Hofstede Insights*

  https://www.hofstede-insights.com/country/the-philippines/

- 'Five must-have qualities of every Filipino business leader', *The Business Advisor*, 5 February 2022

https://www.globe.com.ph/business/enterprise/blog/must-have-qualities-filipino-business-leader.html#gref
- 'Philippines has most women in senior positions', Women in Business report, Grant Thornton insights, 24 Feb 2020

  https://www.grantthornton.com.ph/insights/global-insights1/articles/philippines-has-most-women-in-senior-positions/
- China, Hofstede Insights

  https://www.hofstede-insights.com/country/china/
- Singapore, *Hofstede Insights*

  https://www.hofstede-insights.com/country/singapore/
- Christopher Bruton, 'Women at work: Asian Trends', Bangkok Post, 26 June 2017

  https://www.bangkokpost.com/business/1275951/women-at-work-asian-trends
- Thailand, Hofstede Insights

  https://www.hofstede-insights.com/country/thailand/
- 'Thailand leads the region in women top executives', Royal Thai embassy, Washington DC, 22 March 2019

  https://thaiembdc.org/2019/03/22/thailand-leads-the-region-in-women-top-executives/
- 'Which country works the longest hours?' *BBC, Worklife*, 2018 https://www.bbc.com/worklife/article/20180504-which-country-works-the-longest-hours
- Motoko Rich and Hisako Ueno, 'Shinzo Abe Vowed Japan Would Help Women "Shine". They're Still Waiting'. *The New York Times*, 13 September 2020
- 'Japan's dismal rank in world gender equality shows struggle in political, economic spheres', The Mainichi, 31 March 2021,

(Japanese original by Aya Shiota, Integrated Digital News Center)

- Japan, Hofstede Insights

  https://www.hofstede-insights.com/country/japan/

- India, Hofstede Insights

  https://www.hofstede-insights.com/country/india/

- Women in Business 2021 report, *Grant Thornton International Ltd*, 2021

- Sachin P, Mampatta, 'MNCs lead in women's representation on boards', *Business Standard*, 26 May 2020

  https://www.business-standard.com/article/markets/multinational-companies-lead-in-women-s-representation-on-their-boards-120052600038_1.html

- Shruti Medha, 'Asian firms continue to lag in gender diversity even as investors push for change', *Asian Investor*, 18 October 2021

  https://www.asianinvestor.net/article/asian-firms-continue-to-lag-in-gender-diversity-even-as-investors-push-for-change/473319

Chapter 2

- Lee Min Kok, 'Kiasu is Oxford English Dictionary's Word of the Day: Other Singlish words in the OED', *The Straits Times*, 11 February 2015

  https://www.straitstimes.com/singapore/kiasu-is-oxford-english-dictionarys-word-of-the-day-other-singlish-words-in-the-oed

- WongKimHoh, 'The "tiger mum" who makes HP roar, *The Straits Times*, 21 March, 2021

- Avivah Wittenberg-Cox, 'What do Countries with the best coronavirus responses have in common? Women leaders', *Forbes*, 13 April 2020
- Five must-have qualities of every Filipino business leader, *The Business Advisor*, 5 February 2022

    https://www.globe.com.ph/business/enterprise/blog/must-have-qualities-filipino-business-leader.html#gref

Chapter 3

- Five must-have qualities of every Filipino business leader, *The Business Advisor*, 5 February 2022

    https://www.globe.com.ph/business/enterprise/blog/must-have-qualities-filipino-business-leader.html#gref
- Jack Zenger and Joseph Folkman, 'Research: Women Score Higher Than Men in Most Leadership Skills' *Harvard Business Review*, 25 June 2019

Chapter 5

- Jack Zenger and Joseph Folkman, 'Research: Women Score Higher Than Men in Most Leadership *Skills' Harvard Business Review*, 25 June 2019
- Bartleby, 'A woman's work, *The Economist* March 7th-13th, 2020

Chapter 6

- Whitney Johnson, 'Break Out of the Girls Club', HBR Guide for Women at Work, *Harvard Business Review Press*, 2019

- Anne Welsh McNulty, 'Don't Underestimate the Power of Women Supporting Each Other at Work', *Harvard Business Review*, 3 September 2018
- 'Philippines has most women in senior positions', Women in Business report, *Grant Thornton insights*, 24 Feb 2020

  https://www.grantthornton.com.ph/insights/global-insights1/articles/philippines-has-most-women-in-senior-positions/

Chapter 7

- Walter Sim, 'Japanese society starting to stir in support of gender equality,' *Strait Times*, 22 February 2021

  https://www.straitstimes.com/asia/east-asia/japanese-society-starting-to-stir-in-support-of-gender-equality
- An interview with Deborah Tannen by HBR editors Amy Bernstein, Sarah Green Carmichael, and Nicole Torres, 'How women's Ways of Talking Differ from Men's', HBR Guide for Women at Work, *Harvard Business Review Press*, 2019
- Karen Gilchrist, 'The superpower that led this woman to the top of Twitter's Asia-Pacific business', *CNBC*, 17 Jan 2021

  https://www.cnbc.com/2021/01/18/the-superpower-that-led-maya-hari-to-head-up-twitters-apac-business.html

Chapter 8

- Walter Sim, 'Japanese society starting to stir in support of gender equality,' *Strait Times*, 22 February 2021

  https://www.straitstimes.com/asia/east-asia/japanese-society-starting-to-stir-in-support-of-gender-equality.
- Missing female entrepreneurs, *Japan Times*, 7 March 2019

- https://www.japantimes.co.jp/opinion/2019/03/07/commentary/japan-commentary/missing-female-entrepreneurs/
- Bonnie Chu, 'What is holding women back from the workforce in Asia?', *Forbes*, 30 April 2019

  https://www.forbes.com/sites/bonniechiu/2019/04/30/what-is-holding-women-back-from-the-workforce-in-asia/?sh=3af71bab5a6b
- Jack Zenger and Joseph Folkman, 'Research: Women Score Higher Than Men in Most Leadership *Skills*' *Harvard Business Review*, 25 June 2019
- The glass-ceiling index, 'Go north, young woman', *The Economist*, 7-13 March 2020
- Nirmala Ganapathy, 'Beauty start-up's success spurs India's women entrepreneurs', *The Straits Times*, 29 November 2021

Chapter 10

- Five must-have qualities of every Filipino business leader, *The Business Advisor*, 5 February 2022

  https://www.globe.com.ph/business/enterprise/blog/must-have-qualities-filipino-business-leader.html#gref

Chapter 11

- Jack Zenger and Joseph Folkman, 'Research: Women Are Better Leaders During a Crisis', *Harvard Business Review*, December 30, 2020

Profiles of people in the book

Abanti Sankaranarayanan is chief group public affairs officer and member, group executive board, Mahindra Group, India. She nearly thirty years of experience in two corporate institutions—Diageo and Tata (TAS)—across general management, marketing, public policy, corporate reputation and sustainability. In 2020, she was featured in a Business world list of most influential women who made a 'positive impact on India's economy and society'.

Adele Tao is the leader of LIXIL Water Technology for the Greater China region. With experience spanning over two decades, she has built a robust network with architects, designers and the hospitality industry in China and Hong Kong. Under her leadership, the team has consolidated and expanded market share and improved sales performance. Prior to LIXIL, Adele worked in Philips home appliances, Whirlpool China Investment Co. Ltd., and Kohler.

Atsi Sheth is managing director and global head, Credit Strategy and Research at Moody's Investors Service. Her prior roles have included managing director, Sovereign Risk at Moody's and chief economist, Reliance Capital. Atsi has worked in New York, Singapore and Mumbai, opportunities that have shaped her global perspective on the merits of diversity, equity and inclusion and the multiple ways they enhance business outcome.

Bonita Lee has over twenty-five years of HR experience across Asia Pacific, China and the emerging markets including Southeast Asia, Middle East/Africa and Latin America. She is currently vice president, Human Resources, Emerging Markets for a global pharmaceuticals company. Prior to this, Bonita held a variety of HR leadership positions in global pharmaceuticals and consumer goods companies.

Carol Dominguez is the president and CEO of John Clements Consultants, Inc., a leading recruitment and human resources services firm for shared services and BPO companies operating in the Philippines. She has an extensive history of building exceptional client portfolios in human resource consultancy through strategic approaches, including concept, research and analysis, marketing and sales, and execution.

Chris Ng has progressed through various finance roles and led as business leader at a US consumer goods MNC for Southeast Asia/India region. She has a proven track record in developing sales and channel opportunities, driving profitable and sustainable sales growth, with focus on win-win collaboration with business partners.

Gregory Rastello is an intercultural and leadership coach and talent development professional with twenty-five years of experience in Asia. Originally from France, Gregory has lived and worked in China and Southeast Asia for twenty-five years. He is passionate about crafting leadership development and intercultural programmes, enabling individuals and teams to thrive in diverse and multicultural business environments.

Dr Harpreet A De Singh, the first woman CEO of an Indian airline, has a doctorate in business administration with specialization in Ethical Business Management with Divinity, Purity and Soul Consciousness. As a leader of aviation industry, she has broken numerous glass ceilings. She is a lead auditor of IATA and has served on many international councils of IATA and STAR Alliance.

Jin Montesano is executive officer and chief people officer of LIXIL. She also serves on the board of directors of the LIXIL Corporation. She joined the company in 2014 as chief public affairs officer, leading global communications and corporate responsibility for the company. As chief people officer, she supports LIXIL's transformation from a people and culture perspective. She has lived and worked in Brussels, Singapore, Bangkok and now Tokyo.

Jon E. Kaplan is president, TDS Global Solutions which he founded in 1991 as the first and only full service BPO support company with locations in the United States and the Philippines.

Prior to this, he managed in-house start-up call centres for General Motors and BF Goodrich and worked as Sales VP for a call centre outsourcing company.

Karen Tay Koh started her career at the Ministry of Finance in Singapore. She was Deputy CEO of Singhealth in 2001, and concurrently was Deputy CEO of Singapore General Hospital until 2008, when she retired from her public sector career. Karen has been a board director on several boards in the public, non-profit and private sectors, including Singapore EDB Investments, Northeastern University USA, HSBC Bank Singapore Limited and Banyan Tree Holdings.

Karishma R Phatarphekar is a partner with Deloitte India and leads the Tax Controversy Management team in the area of transfer pricing, corporate and international tax and indirect tax. Prior to joining Deloitte, she worked with renowned accounting and tax firms. She has twenty-three years of experience in transfer pricing, tax dispute management and resolution. Karishma has recently been featured in the list of the top ten transfer pricing advisors in India.

Kumi Ito started her career with Sony Corporation as a marketing specialist and strategist. After being a stay-at-home mom and a contract worker, Kumi resumed working at IBM Japan, and became a partner for a strategic consulting group. In 2014, she joined GE Healthcare Japan as CMO after which she was CEO of 4U Lifecare. Currently, she is a board member of various companies including SOMPO Holding, Fuji Furukawa E&C and Ryohin-Keikaku (MUJI).

Lani Darmawan has thirty-seven years' experience in banking, covering retail, consumer banking, branch banking and digital. She has worked for over twenty years with large banks in Indonesia including Standard Chartered Bank, Citibank and Permata Bank. She joined CIMB Niaga Indonesia in 2016, and took on the role of president director and CEO of CIMB Niaga in December 2021. She is a dentist by education.

Lilian Wu is an experienced multinational human resources management practitioner in pharmaceutical and automotive industries. She specialized in HR business partnership, aligning talent strategy, programmes and solutions with business strategy. Lilian has accomplished various HR missions in China, Asia-Pacific as well as globally. She is passionate about career management, talent and organization development.

Lynette V. Ortiz is the first Filipino CEO of Standard Chartered Bank Philippines. She was previously the regional head of capital markets, ASEAN, based in Singapore. She has had over thirty years of extensive experience starting with Citibank in New York and has held senior roles in risk management, treasury, corporate finance and capital markets in foreign and local institutions.

Dr Marie-Thérèse Claes heads the Institute for Gender and Diversity in organizations at WU Vienna University of Economics and Business. In addition, she holds guest professorships at several other universities in Europe, Asia and the United States of America. She was dean of the Faculty of Business at the Asian University Thailand, and director of the Executive MBA at LSM, University of Louvain.

PROFILES OF PEOPLE IN THE BOOK

Mike Liu is a seasoned executive with over thirty years of experience in digital transformation and market growth strategies with leading technology multinationals. Mike was the former managing director and legal representative for DXC Technology in Greater China region. Prior to that, Mike was the global vice president, country head and legal representative for Infosys in China.

Nayantara Bali currently serves as an independent director on several leading public listed companies across Singapore, India and the UK. She was a senior executive at Procter & Gamble for over twenty-five years in multiple business unit head roles. She is also co-owner/director of ANV Consulting Pte, a boutique management consultancy. She was the first Asian woman member of P&G's Global Business Leadership Council.

Oranuch (Mimee) Lerdsuwankij is the CEO and co-founder of Techsauce, a leading technology/innovation community platform in Thailand. Techsauce also hosts the largest technology conference in Southeast Asia called Techsauce Global Summit. She is recognized as one of the pioneers in building the Thai tech startup ecosystem. She is also interested in bringing technology to help the weaker sections of society.

Pavitra Singh currently heads HR for PepsiCo India. She has been with PepsiCo for over fifteen years. She has held leadership positions in India and other markets across roles such as Talent Management, L&D, Culture, D&I, Talent Acquisition and HR Business partnering roles. An inclusion and diversity evangelist, she strongly believes in creating a culture of inclusion for all diversity to thrive in spirit and action.

Polly Ng is the president and chief executive officer, BWS Group (Aquaculture AI Solutions) and the founder, chairman and CEO of Global Women Connect. She has held global and regional leadership positions such as worldwide sales operations, process director and Asia-Pacific business director of US-based Fortune 500 MNCs, as well as managing director of Chinese based firms. Her experience spins across various digital industries including IT, digital healthcare, digital printing and management consulting.

Pri Notowidigdo is a board advisor, executive coach, and C-suite executive search consultant to multinational corporations, government, donor agencies, non-profit organizations, family businesses, and entrepreneurial enterprises. Over a career spanning forty-five years of global experience, his expertise includes communication, leadership, corporate governance, psychometric assessment and cross-cultural effectiveness.

Punita Kumar-Sinha is a senior investment professional with over thirty years of experience in investment management in emerging and international markets. She has led teams and business units focused on Asian equity funds at Blackstone Asia Advisors, CIBC Oppenheimer, and Batterymarch. Punita is an independent director for several companies and on the board of governors of the CFA Institute.

Purvi Sheth manages India's leading legacy strategic HR consulting firm, Shilputsi Consultants. With over twenty-five years of experience, Purvi has been responsible for the firm's growth as well as the evolution of their practice areas of HR advisory, talent acquisition and leadership development. Purvi is a coach to business and HR leaders on strategic solutions that are congruent with business goals and organizational cultures.

Rakshit Hargave is currently a CEO in the Aditya Birla Group, heading Grasim Paints. Until recently he was based out of Bangkok, heading Nivea, Beiersdorf, for the ASEAN countries, Australia and New Zealand. Prior to this, he was managing director at Nivea, India and has worked with Unilever, Domino's Pizza and Nestle India. He graduated in engineering from the Indian Institute of Technology, BHU and went on to complete his MBA from FMS, New Delhi.

Renuka Ramnath, founder, managing director and CEO of Multiples Alternate Asset Management is one of the most experienced private equity fund managers in India, with a career of over thirty-five years in financial services. She spent eight years as the MD and CEO of ICICI Venture, building it into one of the largest private equity funds in the country. In 2009, she took an entrepreneurial turn and founded Multiples, an India-focused private equity platform.

Renyung Ho is a next generation entrepreneur, impact investor and writer. She currently spearheads Banyan Tree's transformation drive towards developing a digitally forward ecosystem of brands around wellbeing and sustainability. This encompasses ecommerce, customer experience and insights, brand development, as well as innovation workstreams with cross-functional teams for critical change projects. She joined the Group in 2009.

PROFILES OF PEOPLE IN THE BOOK

Dr Rohini Srivathsa is the national technology officer at Microsoft India. In her role, she is responsible for driving innovation and growth through 'tech-intensity' across industry and the government. Rohini began her career in research and development at AT&T Bell Laboratories. She engaged with CxOs across emerging markets during her strategy consulting career at the Boston Consulting Group and IBM Global Business Services.

Roshni Nadar Malhotra is the chairperson of HCLTech, a leading global technology organization and the chairperson of its CSR Board Committee. Roshni is a trustee of the Shiv Nadar Foundation which invests in nation building institutions and driving transformational leadership. Roshni is also the Chairperson and driving force behind VidyaGyan, a leadership academy for the economically underprivileged, meritorious, rural students of Uttar Pradesh.

Senela Jayasuriya is a multi-award-winning CEO of Global, keynote speaker and empowerment coach. She is the founder of Women Empowered Global & 1 Million Women in Power. She is also the Sri Lanka ambassador to the United States Presidential Service Center, focusing on initiatives to promote inclusive workplaces and programmes to promote more women on Boards. She is a strong proponent for diversity and inclusion on a global scale.

Shahrukh Marfatia is director, Asia-Pacific and corporate adviser with White Crow Research and Colvill Banks. He brings to the table extensive hands-on global and regional business experience across Singapore, India, China, Indonesia and Mauritius. Over the years, he has held various senior VP/CHRO level global and regional roles in the Asia-Pacific and Middle East regions.

Shiv Shivakumar has been a CEO for half his career and was one of the youngest CEOS in India. Shiv is group executive president at Aditya Birla Group for strategy and business development. Prior to this, he was chairman and CEO for PepsiCo for four years and before that with Nokia as CEO for India and emerging markets. Shiv is the bestselling author of *The Art of Management* and *The Right Choice*.

Shojiro Mitsuzawa is currently the CFO of a healthcare technology start-up in Japan called Integrity Healthcare. After graduating from university, he worked for a Japanese bank for a few years and later as a management consultant in Accenture's Tokyo office. Subsequently, Shojiro worked for Mitsui & Co. for thirteen years in growth and buy-out investment, including five years as the president of a new business in New York.

Sofia Shakil is director of The Asia Foundation, where she heads the country programme for Pakistan and leads the work on economic development across Asia. Early in her career she worked with international NGOs such as the Aga Khan Development Network and Save the Children, and then spent almost two decades working with the World Bank and the Asian Development Bank.

Sunsanee Supatravanij worked for over eighteen years in Unilever, where she became an expert brand builder and marketer across ten product categories and three continents. Having been responsible for innovation and strategy in Asia, she was assigned to the coporate centre in London and in 2001, Sunsanee was among the first to be appointed global brand director. After leaving Unilever, Sunsanee was CEO of a Thai publicly listed company. She is an independent board director and mentor to start-ups in Thailand.

Dr Susan P. Chen has worked with teams and leaders to develop talent strategies and interventions that build capabilities for sustainable growth across a broad range of companies. Susan has worked with the first decacorn technology platform in Indonesia that went public, a fintech multinational company in Singapore, a national energy company in Norway, and a gaming and entertainment company headquartered in the United States.

Vanitha Narayanan is a senior global executive and board leader with a successful track record spanning three decades in technology and telecommunications. In 2020, Vanitha retired after a career spanning three decades at IBM where she held multiple key roles leading large businesses in the United States, Asia-Pacific and India geographies. These roles included serving as managing director and chairman of IBM India and vice president for the communications sector across Asia-Pacific.

Xu Ge Fei is a self-taught Chinese woman. She left school at the age of sixteen, in her native country. In 2009, Fei created a successful publishing house in Paris 'Les Éditions Fei' to introduce Chinese culture to the French. From 2015 to 2019, Fei was general manager of the Hachette Livre Group's subsidiary in Beijing, China. There she edited, among other things, the Chinese version of the book, *Revolution*, by President Emmanuel

Macron. Since May 2022, she has represented China Publishing E&I Group in Paris.

Yousuke Yagi founded People First Ltd in 2017, an organization that provides professional HR services such as building HR strategy, developing leaders and coaching executives. Prior to this in 2012, Yagi held the positions of executive officer and executive vice president at LIXIL Group Corporation where he led HR to transform the company from domestic to global.

Yurika Kurakata grew up in Japan and Australia, and received degrees from the University of the Sacred Heart in Tokyo, Harvard University and Singapore Management University. With over fifteen years' experience working in education and professional development on East Asia for educators, she is currently based in Seattle, USA.

Acknowledgements

In the book's journey of almost three years, from ideation to publication, I have a long list of people to acknowledge.

Let me begin by thanking the people quoted in the book:

Abanti Sankaranarayanan, Adele Tao, Atsi Sheth, Bonita Lee, Carol Dominguez, Chris Ng, Gregory Rastello, Harpreet A De Singh, Jin Montesano, Jon E. Kaplan, Karen Tay Koh, Karishma R. Phatarphekar, Kumi Ito, Lani Darmawan, Lilian Wu, Lynette V. Ortiz, Marie-Therese Claes, Mike Liu, Nayantara Bali, Oranuch Lerdsuwankij, Pavitra Singh, Polly Ng, Pri Notowidigdo, Punita Kumar-Sinha, Purvi Sheth, Rakshit Hargave, Renuka Ramnath, Renyung Ho, Rohini Srivathsa, Roshni Nadar Malhotra, Senela Jayasuriya, Shahrukh Marfatia, Shiv Shivakumar, Shojiro Mitsuzawa, Sofia Shakil, Sunsanee Supatravanij, Susan P. Chen, Vanitha Narayanan, Xu Ge Fei, Yousuke Yagi and Yurika Kurakata,

A big thank you for sharing your experiences and observations and for trusting me. You all are the stars of this book.

In addition to the above, I had insightful conversations with the following people who shared their varied perspectives:

Joy Padlan, Ambe Tierro, Michelle Pang, Tomoko Takazawa, Shakilla Shahjihan, Priscilla Pangemanan, Selena Kwek, Joyce Jenkins, Khanittha Saeheng, Michael Jenkins, Yu-Ching Chang, Catherine Chauvinc, David Chen, Jacinta Quah, Joanna Guoh, Angela Hsu, Bunn Kasemsup, Ritika Chaudhury and Sarah Walton.

All of your inputs enriched and shaped the narrative in the book. Thank you!

There were many who generously made introductions to people who contributed to the book in some manner, shape or form:

Shiv Shivakumar, Pradeep Pant, Pushkar Misra, Carol Dominguez, Vineet Sahai, Catherine Peyrols Wu, Wanweera Rachdawong, Kartika Sutandi, Anupama Puranik, Wonbae Lee, Emily Davis, Howei Wu, Debjani Ghosh, Murali Rajagopalan, Amit Bhartia, Luluaa Mathias, Mike Liu, Kumi Ito, Karen Tay Koh, Gregory Rastello, Shahrukh Marfatia, Rakshit Hargave, Yurika Kurakata, Pri Notowidigdo, Jin Montesano, Purvi Sheth and Abanti Sankaranarayanan,

I am very grateful for your kindness in graciously connecting me to people you know, many of whom are now a part of this book.

~

It was a conversation with Shiv Shivakumar that sparked the idea and inspiration to write this book. Shiv is a highly accomplished corporate leader whose mentorship I am immensely grateful for. Few leaders give their time, guidance and access to their network

ACKNOWLEDGEMENTS

as generously as Shiv does. He connected me to many of the leaders featured in this book. His support made this journey smoother and richer.

Abanti Sankaranarayanan and Jitania Kandhari were wonderful sounding boards; their interest and enthusiasm prompted me to get from ideation to action.

Meenakshi Sanghi has been incredibly supportive of this book from the beginning. An avid reader well-versed on a variety of subjects, her timely and well-balanced inputs helped hone the initial drafts as well as my confidence. I am grateful for her interest, commitment and friendship.

Leela Abdulwahid painstakingly transcribed lengthy interviews that ran into several pages. To add to the complexity, she had to navigate a range of different accents. I appreciate her professionalism, patience and attention to detail.

Special thanks to Charuvi Misra, for her whole-hearted support and for sharing her views as a young dynamic entrepreneur.

I am grateful to my family for their unconditional support. My husband Amal was a constant sounding board; he shared relevant feedback on the draft chapters and encouraged me throughout. Anushka, my daughter, was my ad-hoc research assistant despite her busy schedule. She also designed most of the visuals in the book, including the creative 'What's in her bag' illustrations.

I am grateful to Purvi Sheth for her enthusiasm to celebrate every milestone and for getting me through some tough times. Anand Sanghi has been a rock-solid pool of creative ideas and affirmative energy. Amit Bhartia and Leena Kelshikar have consistently supported my literary ventures and cheered me on.

I would like to acknowledge my colleagues at SIETAR South East Asia for enriching me with interesting experiences that informed and shaped my writing. Here's to my lovely partners in culture: Joyce Jenkins, Judit Vegh, Seiji Nakano, Greg Rastello, and Marie-Therese Claes.

After I submitted my manuscript, I was in for a surprise when a new editor came on board. I was anxious as to how this would impact the book. I needn't have; Suchismita Ukil was meticulous and supportive. I am grateful for her attention to detail and process and for her insightful and clear perspectives. I would also like to acknowledge Siddhesh Inamdar for his faith in this book and for enabling a smooth transition. Thank you to the fabulous team at HarperCollins: you all made it work!

Index

Abe, Shinzo, 13
Albright, Madeleine, 110
Ardern, Jacinda, 190
Arisa, 2, 69, 123
artificial intelligence (AI), 203
Art of Management, The, Shivakumar, 90
Asian: being, 114–116, 129–130; countries, x, 3–4, 7, 105, 130, 181–182, 204; cultures, 97, 155, 183; leadership, 22, 181, 192; women, 20, 26, 96, 112, 123, 127, 142, 182, 188, see also women; women leaders
Asia-Pacific (APAC), 15–16

Bain & Company, 135
Bali, Nayantara, 31–32, 82, 84, 167
Bhan, Shereen, 90
biases, xi–xii, 14, 86–87, 108–109, 135–136, 141, 143, 183–184; cultural, 145; unconscious, 93, 105, 141, 145, see also stereotyping
bonding 4, 43, 52; "Jie Yuan" 结缘, 61; over food/meals, 81–84, see also networking
business dress. See dress/attire
business process outsourcing (BPO), in Philippines, 4

Chen, Susan P., 62, 64, 86, 149, 171, 182

INDEX

Chief Executive Officers (CEO), 9, 26, 31, 37–38, 41, 43, 59–60, 62, 67–68, 138–139, 195, 200; on managing male ego, 69; role of women in 19; token female, 124
Chief Finance Officer (CFO), 9, 16, 159
China, 5–7; female billionaires, 8
China CEO, Fernandez, 41
Claes, Marie-Therese, 132–133, 142, 185
Clinton, Hillary, 87
collaborative approach, 26, 28, 61, 68
commitments, 60, 76, 78–79, 91, 176
communication, 77, 81, 113–114, 122, 126, 161–162, 206; Ito on, 122; style, 70–71, 151, 154–155, 157, 183
confidence, 116–118
Confucianism, 3, 133
consistency, 77–78, 91
Corporate culture, xiii, 158
Cortes, Anna, 36–38, 94, 112–113
Covid-19 pandemic, xiii, 20, 35, 43, 45, 61, 80–81, 121, 133, 165, 203
creativity, 60, 106, 120

credibility, 21, 58, 74–76, 78, 86, 92, 94, 136, 140, 184
cultures, x, xiii–1, 3–4, 19–20, 32, 34, 48, 63–65, 71–72, 84–85, 102–103, 130, 140, 154–155, 157–158; Asian, 97; in China, 37, 105, French, 105; of harmony in Japan, 122; organization, 104–106; perception in patriarchal, 149; women in Southeast Asian, 134

Darmawan, Lani, 38, 49–51
decision-making, 55, 59, 64–65, 91, 109, 140, 184, 204; ringi in, 65
Detert, James R., 33
digitization, 203
Dominguez, Carol, 44, 94
dress/attire, 87–89, 102

egos, managing, 67–68
emotional intelligence, 45–47
emotions, 6, 43, 49, 51, 122, 192
empathy, 44–45, 47, 49, 53, 55–56, 58, 153, 155, 190, 194, 203, 207

family-owned businesses, 184
female leaders, 67, 71, 85, 97, 99, 106, 109, 152, 171, 174, 178, 181–182, 188,

see also women leaders/leadership
Fernandez, Juan Antonio, 41
Filipinos, 4, 35–36, 42–44, 99, 150, 171
Flynn, Jill, 29

Gallop, Cindy, 187; *gaman* (values in Japanese) 175, see also values
Gates, Melinda, 103–104
gender, 7–8, 71, 74, 100–101, 104, 108–109, 113, 118, 125, 131–132, 187, 191, 203–204; diversity, 15, 125, 134; emancipation, 142; equality 17, 210
Global Women Connect (GWC), 40, 60, 191
Goldsmith, Marshall, 179
Google India, 135
Gopinath, C.Y., 35
Grant Thornton's Women in Business Report, 9, 14–15
guanxi (building relationship), in China, 40–42, 82

Hamaguchi, Keiichiro, 104
hard drive and software, 184–185
Hargave, Rakshit, 11
harmony, x, 3, 23, 72, 116, 122, 182; 'wa' in Japan, 12
HCL Tech, 28, 107
Heath, Kathryn, 29

Helgesen, Sally, 179
hierarchy, x, 1–3, 31, 37, 41, 58–59, 65, 100, 106, 138–139, 151, 153, 182–183; in China, 37
Himari, 116–117, 158, 160, 162
Ho, Renyung, 45, 69–70, 183–184, 187, 191
Hofstede's Cultural Dimensions Model, 6, 181
Holt, Mary Davis, 29
How Women Rise, Helgesen and Goldsmith, 179

hu ma, Mandarin, 24
humility, x, 3, 23, 35–36, 38, 55, 123, 182, 188; as feminine trait, 36
impostor syndrome, 137
inclusiveness, 8, 27, 38, 73, 78, 84–85, 105, 107, 109, 197, 207
India, x–xiii, 3–4, 13–16, 18–19, 47–48, 83, 86, 89–90, 100–101, 145, 151, 168, 203–204
influencing, 57–58, 60, 62, 67, 69–73, 149, 184
information, Vinitha on, 127
Ishikawa, Yumi, 142
Iyer, Shashi, 22

Japan, x–xii, 2, 4, 12–13, 15, 18–19, 83, 100, 105, 133,

140, 142; giri choco culture in, 132; as masculine society, 181; women in, 13, 87, 117, 132, 159, 204; women leaders, 99, 158–160

Jayasuriya, Senela, 20, 28, 76, 193

Kaplan, Jon E., 26, 43, 51, 174
karoshi, in Japan, 13
Kataoka, Emi, 132
Kelan, Elisabeth, 108
kiasu as Hokkien (China), 23–24
Koh, Karen Tay, 10, 59, 114–115, 169–170, 176, 189
Kreng Jai, in Thai culture, 120
Kumar-Sinha, Punita, 88, 98–99, 101, 131, 151, 193
Kumi Ito, 63–64, 122, 124–125, 138–140, 164, 166, 192–193
Kumi-san, 139
Kurakata, Yurika, 12–13, 175
#KuToo movement, 143

leadership: in China, 6; expectations, 181–184; gender-agnostic, xii, 57, 74; Mitsuawa on, 139; Nooyi on, 128; style, 22, 26–27, 41, 45, 50, 52, 55, 101, 104, 107, 168, 188, 191; traditional vs lateral, 63–65; traits, xii, 181

Lee, Bonita, 23, 71–72, 157–158, 172
Lerdsuwankij, Oranuch (Mimee), 80–81, 135, 165–166, 191, 193
Lisa, 186–187
Li Ta 利他 (win-win), 61
Liu, Mike, 7, 42, 51
malasakit, in Philippines, 42, 44
Malhotra, Roshni Nadar, 28, 85, 107, 140–141, 168
Managing Directors (MDs), 9, 19, 124
Mao Zedong, 7–8
Marfatia, Shahrukh, 152, 170
Martha, 106, 158
maternal instincts, 24, 188, 190
Maxwell, John, 186
Meyer, Erin, 64
Mitsuzawa, Shojiro, 139–40, 159
MNC cultures, 71
Molinsky, Andy, 137, 169
Moment of Lift, The, Gates, 103
Montesano, Jin, 65–66, 101–103, 125
Mori, Yoshiro, 122
My Life in Full, Nooyi, 95, 108

Narayanan, Vanitha, 29, 53–55, 78, 80–81, 113, 119, 126–127, 187
nemawashi (going aroud the roots), 66

networking, 63–64, 73, 126–127, 198–199
Ng, Chris, 24–26, 32, 44, 77, 87–88, 91–92, 126, 193
Ng, Polly, 40–41, 60, 153–154, 184, 187, 191
Nooyi, Indra, 75–76, 95, 108, 128
Notowidigdo, Pri, 50, 67, 142

Olivia, 87, 101, 115, 117
Ong, Christina, 189
Onnanoko (Japanese), 159
openness, 120, 203
organization cultures, 104, 134
Ortiz, Lynette V., 26–28, 43, 93, 98–100, 118–119, 124–125, 149–150, 193

Pacquiao, Manny, 36
pakikisama (sense of bonding in Filipinos), 4, see also bonding
patriarchal mindsets, x
perceptions, xi, 34, 50–51, 85–86, 91, 135, 149, 170, 182
Phatarphekar, Karishma R., 166–167
Philippines, x–xi, 4, 4–5, 13, 18–19, 36–38, 42–44, 112, 118, 168, 175
Pinoys. See Filipinos
Power Distance Index (PDI) of Hofsted model, 5–6

prejudices, 75, 90, see also biases
Premuzic, Tomas Chamorro, 187
Pure Soul Quotient (PSQ), 164

Ramnath, Renuka, 52–53
Ranaut, Kangana, 132
Rastello, Gregory, 49, 82, 155, 180
Reach50, Molinsky, 169
relationships, 2–3, 14, 27, 40–44, 50–52, 54, 58, 72, 82, 188–189, 191; building, 2, 41, 58; informal, 48, see also bonding; networking
resilience, 174–175
Rohini, Srivathsa, 60, 77, 157, 188
role models, 104, 126, 128, 145, 189, 206

salutations, 2; of Filipinos, 4
Sankaranarayan/Sankaranarayanan, Abanti, 34–35, 49, 58, 74, 90, 102, 161
senior management, 5, 9, 14–15, 17, 19, 31, 96, 108, 181
sensitivity, 55, 80, 150, 183
Shakil, Sofia, 82, 89, 129–130, 143, 188, 190
Shan Wu 善悟 (understanding challenges), 61

Sheth, Atsi, 145
Sheth, Purvi, 64, 110, 193
Shivakumar, Shiv, 75–76, 90, 134, 142, 180
Shiv Nadar Foundation, 140
Singapore, ix–xi, xiii, 2–4, 8–10, 17–19, 23–24, 26, 41, 44–45, 84–85, 87, 100–101, 123; leaders, 45, 189; women CEO in, 19
Singh, Pavitra, 33, 70, 76, 119, 141, 152–153, 190
skills, xiii, 7, 68, 72–73, 102, 140, 167, 203, 207
speaking up, 22, 84–85, 113–114, 119, 124, 127, 141, 151, 160, 182, 203
Srivathsa, Rohini, 39, 47, 60
stakeholders, 37–38, 51, 58, 66, 72–73, 75, 140
stereotyping, 20, 23, 114, 141, 144, 170, see also biases
Supatravanij, Sunsanee, 33, 96–97, 105, 110, 113, 120–121, 155, 188

Tan, Rosie, 189
Tao, Adele, 37–38, 52–53, 115, 156–157, 172
Taoism, 155–156
Thailand, x–xii, 1–2, 4, 10–13, 15, 18–19, 80, 82, 120, 123, 170–171, 179, 181; as feminine society, 181; women CEO in, 19

tradition, x, 10, 102, see also culture; values
traits, 55, 77, 79, 174, 178, 181, 184, 195, 197, 203, 206
transparency, 31, 80–81

values, x, 3, 5, 10, 12, 21–22, 35, 54–55, 60–61, 67–68, 70, 77, 187–188, 192–193, 202–203
Velloor, Ravi, 91
vulnerability, 31, 33–34; Abanti on, 34–35

women, 15, 185; on Boards, 17–19; in China, 7–8, 116, 132, 146, 156; Claes on, 133; in India, 48, 134; in Indonesia, 133; in Japan, 132; leadership in India, 14, 34; managers, 13, 49, 69, 106, 122, 136, 193; in Philippines, 5; representation, 16–17; in senior roles, 1, 13, 15–16, 44; in Singapore, 9; in South Asia, 143; as successful, xi, 7, 146, 162, 184; in Thailand, 10–11, 116; Xu Ge Fei on, 8
Women Empowered Global, 20, 76, 193
women leaders/leadership, xii, 17, 26–28, 31, 43, 48–51,

55–57, 67–68, 104–106, 113, 118, 121, 126–127, 140, 146, 157–158, 161, 170, 174, 178–181, 187–191, 193–194, 203–204, 207; attributes of, 195–197; in China, 42; in Japan, 159; Koh on, 10; navigate, 130, 149; Ng on, 184–185; in Philippines, 44; and risk taking, 186; successful, x, 160, 162, 182, 206; strategies of, 149–155; in Thailand, 12; as too powerful, 149
working women in Asia, 3, 127, 162, see also women leaders
Wu, Lilian, 61, 105, 173, 187

Xu Ge Fei, 8, 68, 116, 156–157

Yagi, Yousuke, 104–105, 160, 174

Zedong, Mao, 7

About the author

Aarti Kelshikar is an intercultural coach and author. She is the founder of 3A Consulting and has been working in the space of leadership and cultural effectiveness since 2008. She has worked and lived in India, Singapore and the Philippines.

Aarti is a certified facilitator of Cultural Intelligence (CQ) and accredited coach of The International Profiler (TIP), frameworks that help assess and develop intercultural effectiveness. She is also a certified executive coach from the international Neuro Leadership group. Through her cultural interventions, Aarti enables executives and students to successfully transition roles, levels and geographies.

Aarti conducts workshops on topics ranging from developing cultural intelligence and honing a global mindset to doing business in Southeast Asia and India. She has trained senior executives from multinational corporations like Nestlé, Unilever,

ABOUT THE AUTHOR

Proctor and Gamble, Colgate Palmolive, and Texas Instruments to work more effectively in different roles and countries. She also helps organizations achieve greater alignment and synergy across their diverse teams.

Her first book *How India Works: Making Sense of a Complex Corporate Culture* was published in 2018. The book is a guide to the cultural nuances and complexities of working with Indians.

She is on the founding board of SIETAR (Society for Intercultural Education, Training and Research) Southeast Asia. Before discovering the fascinating world of intercultural coaching, Aarti worked for seven years in the area of securities market compliance with the Securities and Exchange Board of India in Mumbai and with ComplianceAsia, a consulting firm in Singapore.

Aarti has a master's in business administration from Narsee Monjee Institute of Management Studies in Mumbai and a bachelor's in commerce from Sydenham College in Mumbai.

30 Years *of* HarperCollins *Publishers* India

At HarperCollins, we believe in telling the best stories and finding the widest possible readership for our books in every format possible. We started publishing 30 years ago; a great deal has changed since then, but what has remained constant is the passion with which our authors write their books, the love with which readers receive them, and the sheer joy and excitement that we as publishers feel in being a part of the publishing process.

Over the years, we've had the pleasure of publishing some of the finest writing from the subcontinent and around the world, and some of the biggest bestsellers in India's publishing history. Our books and authors have won a phenomenal range of awards, and we ourselves have been named Publisher of the Year the greatest number of times. But nothing has meant more to us than the fact that millions of people have read the books we published, and somewhere, a book of ours might have made a difference.

As we step into our fourth decade, we go back to that one word – a word which has been a driving force for us all these years.

Read.